THE ULTIMATE GRILL BIBLE

SERENA FOSTER

ISBN: 9798386811969
10 9 8 7 6 5 4 3 2 1

Index

INTRO

An outdoor gas griddle is an option to be used while camping. It is a device that burns natural gas in order to heat up the metal cooking surface. Its metal surface heats up faster as compared with standard cast iron cookware and since it's metal, it can tolerate high temperatures without burning or charring food. This makes outdoor griddles convenient because they can use them while cooking on a campfire or using other alternative fuels like propane, alcohol, or wood.

The outdoor gas grill is a three-piece design consisting of a large grilling surface, two ovens, and a warming area. The griddle is the term for the flat cooking surface. The entire unit must be placed outdoors on a concrete or brick base. This type of grill requires an open flame at all times for use and it can be powered by natural gas or liquid propane (LP). For safety precautions, it should also have an electronic ignition system.

To use the outdoor gas griddle, you will need to take proper care as well as perform periodic maintenance in order to get optimal results. If you need to replace any parts, it is important to have a list of what types of parts are needed in order to replace them. The more you take care of your grill, the longer it will last and the better-quality cooking experience you will have with it.

The outdoor gas grill is used outdoors on a raised brick or concrete base. The grill is placed directly on the base and the burners are then turned on. Once there is an open flame, adjust the temperature knob and cooking grates so that the unit can be used for cooking or warming foods. The warming compartment acts as an oven for keeping food hot without drying it out.

The outdoor gas griddle is very versatile and can be used for grilling, broiling, smoking and warming food. The range of temperatures that can be attained is quite high compared to other gas grills. In addition to the grill grates, there are also the hinged cooking grates on the lower ovens which makes it easy to get rid of unwanted fat that fall on the plate. The two ovens allow you to use them separately. For a complete cooking experience, you will also need a smoker accessory kit. With this accessory kit you are able to smoke food at your desired temperature as well as low or high temperature.

Benefits of Outdoor Gas Griddle

There are plenty of different types of outdoor griddles available. They have different features and designs. Whatever type of outdoor griddle you choose to use, there are numerous benefits to using them during camping. Below are some useful tips:

It is versatile in cooking – You can use it while barbecuing or cooking inside your tent because it comes in a variety of designs and sizes. You can even bring it with you on your next picnic or park visit if you want to cook anything that requires a stove or grill. A good outdoor gas griddle will have a high cooking surface, which allows you to cook numerous items at the same time. It also comes with handles that add to the comfort of using it.

It is easier on your body – You will not have any issues with your back or neck while using an outdoor griddle. A good gas stove can reach a very high temperature and maintain it without the risk of burning or charring food. This makes it easier to cook while outdoors because you can manipulate temperatures without worrying about burns.

It is safe and easy to clean – Most models are made from stainless steel and other strong materials, which make them durable and efficient for cooking outside. You will not have to worry about it breaking or rusting, which will make cleaning a lot easier. In addition, stainless steel cookware is non-porous and will not absorb odor but instead quickly release it.

It saves space – Most griddles are made with a flat surface that can sit directly on the ground. This lowers the total height of the cooking apparatus, which means you do not need to find room for it inside your camping trailer or camper. You can lay them directly on your deck or porch without worrying about toppling over as you cook.

It is lightweight – An outdoor gas griddle is very light in weight and compact in size. This makes it easier to carry around while traveling. Its portable design makes it one of the best choices for camping enthusiasts who prefer gas stoves over propane or charcoal grills.

Chapter 1.   Prepare Grill To Start Cooking

Preparing the outdoor gas griddle is a very important step. Keep some things in mind to keep your cooking enjoyable.

Read the instructions in the manual. Find out how to adjust the valve, configure the heaters and grease tray, and calibrate thermometer, etc. Make sure you have enough propane on hand to cook over lunch hour or even more than one day of meals if necessary! Check that all connections are tight and secure then fire up your griddle! Check it constantly as it rises temperature so that it does not catch fire or warp prematurely; cool with water only if needed.

If you have used the griddle for longer then a few days, you will probably need to clean it occasionally. Even if your griddle is well-cared for and requires little maintenance, you may still want to wipe down your appliance from time to time. A clean griddle is less likely to have rust caused by spilled oil or grease and burning pellets, which can damage the surface of the griddle.

A gas griddle is designed to cook on the outdoor grill. For outdoor cooking, a metal cover is typically placed over the burner to prevent water from dripping onto the flame and causing a fire. When preparing for outdoor cooking, many people make a mistake of not placing any metal cover on the stove burner when it's supposed to be placed during cooking. Without this protection, gas canisters will burn up quickly and are often abandoned before they have as much time in use as they're allowed by law. To prevent this issue, place an inexpensive aluminum foil ball over top of your burner before you start to cook. This will help protect the burner from water, and will prolong the lifetime of your gas canister.

Gas griddles can sometimes be difficult to start. If a gas griddle is overly rusted or dirty, you may not be able to get it to light. This can make cooking outdoors very difficult! To start your griddle, first make sure that your intended cooking surface is clean and dry. Rocks or other debris can interrupt the flow of gas. Next, place one sparker on the burner of your griddle and then light it with a lighter or match. After waiting for a moment for the flame to flicker consistently (a minute or two), place another sparker on top of this one. You can then turn the griddle on using the knobs or by releasing pressure on the knob.

How to keep your gas grill in tip-top shape?

There are a number of tasks that you can do to help extend the life of your gas grill and make it work better than ever. Some people just simply use their gas grill once or twice a year, but others are more diligent about maintaining their equipment.

Chapter 2.   Tips For Improving Cooking

There are many people that are doing outdoor cooking nowadays. And no matter the kind of cooking you do, griddles can be a good investment because they create such smooth and even cooking surfaces on your grill. This can make a great difference when it comes to drawing out the flavors inside meats and vegetables, as well as crisping up breads and pastries. But griddles still require an occasional brushing of oil or fat in order to keep them from sticking in places and causing food to stick to them as well.

First, you should do some research on griddles so that you can determine the best kind of griddle to purchase. If you are going to be cooking large amounts of food, you might want a larger model. If small amounts of food is all that is needed, a smaller model may work better for your needs. Just like with any tool or appliance, it can work well in one situation and poorly in another.

Secondly, get out there and try out griddles yourself before making a large investment in one. Use recipes from this cook book and experiment to see how the different brands compare when cooking different types of things. This can help you determine what model will serve you best and narrow down your search for the perfect griddle.

Thirdly, keep it clean once it has been used. Just like a regular grill, grease will become an issue if food is not taken care of before it cools down. If this grease is not removed the griddle surface will eventually become unusable and wasted, so ensure to clean the grill after you use. Wiping it down with a damp cloth can work well depending on how much grease there is. If there is residue that builds up in some places using a griddle scraper might be necessary to get every last bit of grease off of it. You may want to invest in a griddle scraper for this use.

Finally, be sure to store your griddle properly when it is not in use. Griddles take up a lot of space so it may be a good idea to purchase a storage case that can be used. If you have purchased more than one griddle, you will have to make some decisions on what to do with the ones that are not being used regularly as your needs change and as you begin purchasing more supplies and equipment. Once they sit for an extended period of time they can become damaged, or hard to use depending on the model you buy.

Chapter 3.   Which Tools To Use

There are many different tools that can be used to clean your outdoor gas griddle. The most common tools are a wire brush, a scrubber and sandpaper. There are also some other hand tools that can be used to help clean the griddle more effectively such as: an old toothbrush, tweezers and cotton swabs. These tools should be cleaned separately before use to prevent cross contamination of bacteria between them.

Besides these standard cleaning tool there is also one more important thinking tool that you might want to consider using in order to make your outdoor gas griddle look like new again - oven cleaner. If you are thinking about using an oven cleaner to clean your outdoor gas griddle please think again! Oven cleaners are in most cases extremely toxic and can contain quite a high percentage of chemicals like hydrochloric acid and lye. This is not something that should be used on a regular basis as it will wear off the protective layer of your griddle.

The best things that you can use to clean the mess from your outdoor gas griddle is soap, hot water and a soft sponge. If your outdoor gas griddle is in good condition you can also use baking soda, some hot water and soap to give your griddle a nice sparkle. Also make sure to use rubber gloves when doing any cleaning as you might come in contact with some of the chemicals that are inside the griddle.

Detergents like dishsoap, laundry detergent and dishwasher detergent can be used on the griddle surface to remove grease, oil and food crumbs. This is also a great way to clean in between the heating elements and underneath the surface where there might be some rust hiding. It's great if you can find rollers for your outdoor gas griddle or a "griddle too." These rollers are very useful in protecting your outdoor gas griddle from any moisture buildup under them.

If any of your food caught on fire and left some burnt spots you can use them to bake a cake on this area. This will help in removing the burnt area. Use hot water and soap to clean the rest of the outdoor gas griddle after using oven cleaner.

Chapter 4. Tips For Cleaning Your Outdoor Gas Griddle

Always use rubber gloves when working with your outdoor gas griddle as it can get covered with bacteria or oil that you might accidently leave behind. Make sure to clean under the rollers when you're done as food particles might be stuck there as well. Cleaning also works best if it's done while the griddle is still warm, but not hot enough to burn you. If you're in a rush make sure to use hot water, soap and a sponge.

Make sure to clean your griddle thoroughly before and after it is used. The best way to do this is by using different kind of cleaning tool for different areas of the griddle.

If you want to get your griddle looking brand new again try using an oven cleaner in order to clean away any dirt and such that might have accumulated on it. This way you can maintain its nice shiny appearance for longer as well. It's important that you follow the directions carefully when using this product so as not to get yourself in trouble with any dangerous chemicals inside the oven cleaner that can be dangerous for your health if ingested.

If you want to use a cleaner that can be used for both the inside and outside of your griddle make sure to use a cleaner that's made for stainless steel. This way you don't need to buy two different types of cleaners.

To remove the smell from your outdoor gas griddle you can scrub it with warm, soapy water. If this doesn't work you can also fill the sink with warm water and baking soda and scrub the surface of your griddle; this way you will also get rid of any grease buildup on your griddle while cleaning it at the same time.

Never use iron on (or anything that makes an iron sound) to clean your outdoor gas griddle as it can damage it. Cleaning with a wire brush is your best choice. If you do this you should always wear gloves so as not to accidently touch the inside of the griddle or the heating elements to avoid any harmful bacteria from being transferred onto you and causing an infection.

Make sure that you rinse the surface of your griddle after using an oven cleaner. The reason is because this type of cleaner has a lot of chemicals in it and may not be easy to remove if left on too long before rinsing off.

When cleaning your griddle always remove the rollers first before you start in order to make it easier. The rollers are often very dirty as they are often covered with grease and oil over time, so it's a great idea to clean them before using any type of cleaner.

Don't leave any moist or damp items under the surface of your outdoor gas griddle as this can cause rust or harm the surface of your griddle over time. Any greasy substances should be wiped off while they are still warm or at least use hot water and soap to help remove them better.

Always soak porous items such as griddle covers or rollers for a short period of time before you use any detergent in order to remove any grease, food crumbs and so on from them. This will prevent them from being damaged when in contact with the detergent. Once you are done cleaning them use hot water and soap to clean them off completely for best results.

If your griddle is over 2 years old it's a great idea to do an total check of your griddle in order to make sure that it's functioning properly and is safe for use. This check can also extend the life of your griddle by some time.

Chapter 5.   Breakfast

1. Caprese Omelet

Prep: Ten min

Cook: Ten min

Serves: 2

Ingredients:

- 6 eggs
- 3 oz. cherry tomatoes, cut in halves
- 1 tbsp fresh basil
- 5 oz. mozzarella cheese, sliced
- Pepper
- Salt

Directions:

1. Pre-heat the griddle to med-low heat
2. Whisk eggs in a container with pepper and salt. Stir in basil.
3. Spray griddle top with cooking spray.
4. Add tomatoes on hot griddle top and sauté for a few mins.
5. Pour egg mixture on top of tomatoes and wait until eggs are slightly firm.
6. Add mozzarella cheese slices on top and let the omelet set.
7. Plate it and have fun.

Nutrition

Cal: 515; Pro: 37 g; Fat: 40 g; Carbs: 5.2 g

2. Cheesy Ham and Pineapple Sandwich

Prep: Ten min

Cook: Twenty min

Serves: 4

Ingredients:

- (10 ounces) package deli sliced ham
- Pineapple rings
- Slices Swiss cheese
- 8 slices of thick bread
- Butter, softened, for brushing

Directions:

1. All of the bread pieces should be butter-side down, and the griddle should be heated to medium.
2. On top of each piece of bread, stack 1/4 of the ham, a pineapple ring, and 1 slice of cheese.
3. Place the sandwiches on the griddle and top with the second slice of bread.
4. Cook the bottom piece of bread until it turns light brown, then flip it over and cook the top slice of bread until it also turns golden brown.

Nutrition:

Cal: 594; Pro: 47.7 g; Fat: 40.3 g; Carbs: 4.7 g

3. Easy Banana Pancakes

Prep: Ten min

Cook: Ten min

Serves: 6

Ingredients:

- 2 eggs
- Vanilla protein powder 2 tbsp
- 1 large banana, mashed
- baking powder 1/8 tsp

Directions:

1. Pre-heat the griddle to medium-low heat.
2. Add all items to the bowl and stir thoroughly to blend while you wait.
3. Apply cooking spray to the griddle's surface.
4. To make a pancake, pour 3 tbsp of batter onto the heated griddle surface.
5. Cook pancake until both sides are just beginning to brown.
6. Serve and relish.

Nutrition:

Cal: 79; Fat: 1.6 g; Pro: 11 g; Carbs: 5.5 g

4. Savory Chicken Burgers

Prep: Ten min

Cook: Twenty min

Serves: 3

Ingredients:

- 1 lb. ground chicken
- garlic powder 1 tsp
- salt 1/2 tsp
- vegetable oil 3 tbsp

- 3 potato buns, toasted
- Half red onion, finely chopped
- onion powder 1/2 tsp
- black pepper 1/4 tsp

Directions:

1. Combine the ground chicken, onion, garlic and onion powder, pepper, and salt in a large bowl. Blend well. Make three equal patties out of the chicken mixture. The mixture shouldn't be overworked to avoid making the burgers too thick.
2. Griddle heat should be set to medium-high. Add the vegetable oil.
3. The chicken patties should be cooked for 5 mins on each side, or until they reach 165°F, after the oil is shimmering.
4. Before placing the patties on the toasted buns, take out the patties from the griddle and let them rest for five mins.

Nutrition:

Cal: 420; Pro: 44.2 g; Fat: 24.8 g; Carbs: 2.8 g

5. Classic American Burger

Prep: Fifteen min

Cook: Thirty-Five min

Serves: 6

Ingredients:

- 2 lb. ground beef, at least 20% fat

- Kosher salt

- One sliced tomato
- One yellow or red onion, sliced
- One head iceberg lettuce, cut into flats
- Thick pieces of American or medium cheddar cheese
- Seeded buns or potato buns, toasted
- Black pepper

Directions:

1. Divide the ground beef into 6 equals loosely formed balls. Press the balls on a flat surface to make patties. Do not overwork them.
2. Open-handedly season the patties with salt and black pepper.
3. Heat your griddle to medium-high.
4. Put the patties on the griddle and press down to ensure that the surface makes contact. Cook for three to four mins.
5. Flip the patties and top with cheese. Cook an additional three to four mins. The cheese should melt by then.
6. Remove the burgers from the griddle and place them on the buns. Top with lettuce, tomato, and onion, as well as your favorite condiments.

Nutrition:

Cal: 410; Pro: 53.4 g; Fat: 18.8 g; Carbs: 4.1 g

6. Turkey Pesto Panini

Prep: Five min

Cook: Six min

Serves: 2

Ingredients:

- One tbsp olive oil
- Three slices French bread
- One avocado, split, seeded, peeled, and sliced
- pesto sauce 1/2 cup
- Four slices mozzarella cheese
- 2 cups chopped leftover turkey
- 1 Roma tomato, thinly sliced

Directions:

1. Pre-heat griddle to medium-high heat.

2. Brush every slice of bread with olive oil on one side.

3. Place 2 slices with the olive oil side down on the griddle.

4. On one side of the French bread, spread 2 tbsp of pesto.

5. To assemble a sandwich, place one piece of mozzarella on the bottom, followed by slices of turkey, tomatoes, avocado, then a second slice of mozzarella. Repeat with the rest of the slices of bread.

6. Cook for two to three minutes per side, or until the bread is browned and the cheese has melted.

7. Warm up and serve with your preferred salad or soup.

Nutrition:

Cal: 1129; Pro: 73 g; Fat: 70.9 g; Carbs: 53.2 g

7. Spinach Pancakes

Prep: Ten min

Cook: Ten min

Serves: 6

Ingredients:

- One cup coconut milk
- One cup spinach, chopped
- One tsp baking soda
- coconut flour 1/2 cup
- black pepper 1/2 tsp
- ground nutmeg 1/2 tsp
- salt 1/2 tsp
- chia seeds 1/4 cup
- Four eggs

Directions:

1. The eggs and coconut milk should be whisked together until they form a frothy.

2. All dry ingredients should be combined before adding the egg mixture and whisking until smooth.

3. Add spinach and thoroughly stir.

4. Set the griddle's heat to medium-low.

5. Apply cooking spray to the griddle's surface.

6. Make a circular pancake by adding 3–4 tbsp of batter on the heated griddle surface.

7. Cook pancakes until they are just beginning to become golden brown.

8. Serve and have fun.

Nutrition:

Cal: 111; Pro: 6.3 g; Fat: 7 g; Carbs: 5 g

8. Cauliflower Hash Browns

Prep: Ten min

Cook: Ten min

Serves: 6

Ingredients:

- One egg
- Three cups cauliflower, grated
- garlic powder 1/4 tsp
- pepper 1/8 tsp
- cheddar cheese 3/4 cup
- cayenne pepper 1/4 tsp
- salt 1/2 tsp

Directions:

1. Pre-heat the griddle to medium-low heat.
2. Mix thoroughly after adding all ingredient to the bowl.
3. Apply cooking spray to the griddle's top.
4. Make 6 hash browns from mixture and place on hot griddle top and cook until brown from both sides.
5. Serve and relish.

Nutrition:

Cal: 80; Fat: 5 g; Pro: 5 g; Carbs: 3 g

9. Chocolate Pancake

Prep: Ten min

Cook: Ten min

Serves: 4

Ingredients:

- Two eggs
- Two tbsp water
- One tsp nutmeg
- Two tbsp erythritol
- One tsp cinnamon
- baking powder 1/2 tsp
- cocoa powder 1 ½ tbsp
- ground flaxseed 1/4 cup
- salt 1/4 tsp

Directions:

1. In a bowl, mix ground flaxseed, baking and cocoa powder, erythritol, spices, and salt.
2. Add eggs and stir well.
3. Add water and stir until batter is well combined.
4. Pre-heat the griddle to medium-low heat.
5. Spray griddle top with cooking spray.
6. Pour a large spoonful of batter on a hot griddle top and make a pancake.
7. Cook pancake for 3–4 mins on each side.
8. Serve and relish.

Nutrition:

Cal: 138; Pro: 4.5 g; Fat: 12 g; Carbs: 11 g

10. Pork Tenderloin Sandwiches

Prep: Ten min

Cook: Twenty-Five min

Serves: 6

Ingredients:

- One tbsp barbecue sauce
- One tsp dry mustard
- 2 (3/4-lb.) pork tenderloins
- One tsp garlic powder
- One tsp sea salt
- One whole-wheat hamburger buns
- 1/2 tsp coarsely ground pepper
- Olive oil, for brushing

Directions:

1. Stir the garlic, salt, pepper, and mustard together in a small mixing bowl.

2. Rub pork tenderloins evenly with olive oil, then seasoning mix.

3. After preheating a griddle to medium heat, cook the meat for 10 to 12 minutes each side, or until a meat thermometer inserted into the thickest part reads 155 degrees Fahrenheit.

4. Remove from griddle and let it rest for 10 mins.

5. Slice thinly, and evenly distribute onto hamburger buns.

6. Sprinkle each sandwich with barbecue sauce and serve.

Nutrition:

Cal: 372; Pro: 37.2 g; Fat: 13.4 g; Carbs: 24.7 g

11. Simple Cheese Sandwich

Prep: Ten min

Cook: Ten min

Serves: 1

Ingredients:

- 2 bread slices
- 2 tsp butter
- 2 cheese slices

Directions:

1. Pre-heat the griddle to medium-low heat.

2. Place cheese slices on top of one bread slice and cover cheese with another bread slice.

3. Spread butter on top of both the bread slices.

4. Cook the sandwich on a heated griddle top until the bread is browned and the cheese has melted.

5. Serve and have fun.

Nutrition:

Cal: 340; Pro: 15.4 g; Fat: 26 g; Carbs: 9.8 g

Chapter 6.   Lunch

12. Garlic Soy Pork Chops

Prep: Twenty min

Cook: One hour

Serves: 4 to 6

Ingredients:

- olive oil 1/2 cup
- soy sauce 1/2 cup
- black pepper 1/2 tsp
- Four cloves of garlic, chopped
- garlic powder 1/2 tsp
- salt 1/2 tsp
- butter 1/4 cup
- 4 to 6 pork chops

Directions:

1. Combine the garlic, soy sauce, olive oil, & garlic powder in a big zip lock bag. Place the pork chops in the marinade and ensure they are well coated. Allow 30 mins for preparation.
2. Pre-heat your griddle at medium-high. Add two tbsp of oil and two tbsp of butter to the griddle.
3. Place the chops on the griddle one at a time, being careful not to crowd them. Cook the chops for around 5 mins on the griddle with additional 2 tbsp of butter. Cook for another 4 mins.
4. After taking the chops from the griddle, brush them with the leftover butter. Serve after five mins of resting.

Nutrition:

Cal 398, Fat 38g, Pro 14g, Carbs 4g

13. Butterflied Chicken

Prep: Fifteen min

Cook: Fifty min

Serves: 6

Ingredients:

- Three tbsp Mexican chili powder
- Three tbsp fresh lime juice
- Salt and ground black pepper, as required
- Two tsp lime zest, freshly grated
- Two tbsp extra-virgin olive oil
- One tsp ground cumin
- One tsp ground coriander
- One tbsp garlic, minced
- One (3½-4-pound) whole chicken, neck and giblets removed

Directions:

1. Arrange the chicken onto a large cutting board, breast side down.
2. Start at the thigh and cut down one side of the backbone using kitchen shears to flip the bird around.
3. Now remove the backbone by cutting along the other side.
4. Change the side, spread it open like a book, and then forcefully flatten the backbone.
5. Combine lime juice, oil, garlic, lime zest, chile powder, coriander, cumin, salt, and black pepper in a clean glass bowl.
6. Apply the spice mixture evenly to the chicken.
7. Refrigerate the chicken for about 24 hours while it is wrapped in plastic.
8. Pre-heat half of the Outdoor Gas Griddle to medium-high heat and leave the remaining half of griddle unheated.
9. Place the chicken with the marinade on the Pre-heated griddle, skin side down and cook for about 5 mins.
10. Cook the chicken for about 5 mins on the other side.
11. The chicken should now be placed on the griddle's unheated side and covered with the cooking dome.
12. Cook for around 30 to 40 mins, or until well cooked.
13. Take the chicken from the griddle and set aside for 10 mins on a dish before cutting.
14. Serve the chicken after slicing it into the desired size pieces.

Nutrition:

Cal 507, Fat 17.1 g, Carbs 0.8 g, Pro 82.2 g

14. Honey Mustard Chicken Drumsticks

Prep: Ten min

Cook: Thirty min

Serves: 8

Ingredients:

- Three garlic cloves, minced
- Dijon mustard ¼ cup
- Two tbsp mustard powder
- Ground black pepper, as required
- Two tbsp low-sodium soy sauce
- Four pounds chicken drumsticks
- honey 1/3 cup

Directions:

1. Garlic, the remaining ingredients, and all but the chicken drumsticks should be mixed together in a dish.
2. Coat the chicken drumsticks generously with spice mixture.
3. Cover the bowl of chicken drumsticks and refrigerate to marinate for at least 2 hours.
4. Pre-heat the Outdoor Gas Griddle to medium-high heat.
5. Grease the griddle.
6. While saving the marinade, remove the chicken drumsticks from the bowl.
7. Cook the chicken drumsticks on the griddle for about 25 to 30 mins, flipping them over and basting them with the marinade every five mins.
8. Serve hot.

Nutrition:

Cal 448, Pro 63.8 g, Fat 14.1 g, Carbs 13.7 g

15. Garlic Spiced BBQ Tenderloin

Prep: Ten min

Cook: Fifteen min

Serves: 4

Ingredients:

- BBQ seasoning
- 1 pork tenderloin, silver skin removed & dried

For the fresh herb sauce:

- ¼ tbsp of garlic powder
- ½ tbsp of kosher salt

- 1 handful of basil, fresh
- ¼ cup of olive oil

Directions:

1. Pre-heat your Blackstone griddle at Medium temperature.
2. Coat the pork in BBQ spice and roast it on the griddle over indirect heat. To achieve consistent cooking, turn the meat frequently.
3. Cook until the food reaches a temperature of 145°F. The steak should be taken from the griddle and let to cool for about 10 mins.
4. The herb sauce will be created by combining all of the sauce ingredients in a food processor. Once or twice more until everything is finely chopped.
5. Sliced diagonally, the pork should be served with the sauce spooned on top. Serve & have fun.

Nutrition:

Cal 183, Fat 7g, Pro 27g, Carbs 2g

16. Lemony Chicken Breast

Prep: Fifteen min

Cook: Sixteen min

Serves: 6

Ingredients:

- fresh lemon juice ¼ cup
- One garlic clove, minced
- Two pounds boneless, skinless chicken breasts
- Salt and ground black pepper, as required
- olive oil ½ cup

Directions:

1. For marinade: in a large bowl, add the oil, lemon juice, garlic, salt, and black pepper and beat until well combined.
2. Put the chicken breasts and marinade in a large plastic bag that can be sealed.
3. Seal the bag and shake it to coat well.
4. Refrigerate overnight.
5. Pre-heat the Outdoor Gas Griddle to medium heat.

6. Grease the griddle generously.
7. Take the chicken breasts out of the bag, then throw away the marinade.
8. A cooking dome should be placed over the chicken breasts after they are on the griddle.
9. Cook for 6 to 8 mins on each side.
10. Serve hot.

Nutrition:

Cal 434, Fat 28.1 g, Carbs 0.4 g, Pro 43.9 g

17. Grilled Rib-Eye Steak

Prep: Fifteen min

Cook: Twenty min

Serves: 4

Ingredients:

- 4 sprigs of rosemary
- Salt & pepper to taste
- 4 ribs of beef (10 oz. each)
- Olive oil to taste
- 4 cloves of garlic

Directions:

1. Remove any excess fat from the beef ribs by washing and drying them.
2. The rosemary should be washed and dried before being chopped finely.
3. Garlic cloves should be peeled and washed before being chopped.
4. The chopped rosemary, garlic, salt, and pepper should all be combined in a mixing bowl.
5. Pre-heat your Blackstone griddle at 350°F and prepare your Blackstone for the direct cooking.
6. After brushing the ribs using olive oil, sprinkle a mixture of rosemary & garlic over the entire surface.
7. Put the meat on the griddle, cover, and cook for around 15 mins, or till the internal temperature has reached 131°F.
8. Turn the meat after 3 mins.
9. Remove the meat out from the griddle after it has finished cooking and set it aside to rest for 5 mins.
10. Place the ribs on serving dishes & serve after 5 mins.

Nutrition:

Cal 420, Fat 29g, Pro 60g, Carbs 2g

18. Simple and Easy Grilled Pork Tenderloin

Prep: Ten min

Cook: Four hours

Serves: 6

Ingredients:

- 1 batch of Pork Rub
- 2 (around 1-pound/454 g) pork tenderloins

Directions:

1. Pre-heat your Blackstone griddle at 250°F and apply a thin layer of oil on the griddle.
2. Season the tenderloins well using the rub. Work the rub into the meat using your hands.
3. Put the tenderloins directly on the griddle and cook for around 4 to 5 hours, or till they reach 145°F (63°C) internal temperature.
4. Remove the tenderloins out from the griddle & set them to rest for 5–10 mins before slicing thinly & serving.

Nutrition:

Cal 364, Fat 22g, Pro 37g, Carbs 3g

19. Sausage and Pineapple Skewers

Prep: Fifteen min

Cook: Ten min

Serves: 4

Ingredients:

- 1 tsp of chopped chives
- 14 oz. of pineapple pulp
- Salt & pepper to taste
- 14 oz. of sausage
- Two tbsp of balsamic vinegar
- Olive oil to taste
- Two tbsp of mustard
- Two tsp of honey

Directions:

1. Wash & dry the pineapple before cutting it into pieces.
2. Cut the sausage into the same size cubes as the pineapple.
3. Alternately place meat cubes and pineapple cubes into the skewers to make the skewers.
4. Prepare the marinating sauce in the meantime.
5. Combine the mustard, vinegar, salt, honey, oil, chives, & pepper in a large-sized mixing dish.
6. The skewers should be put in the dish, covered with plastic wrap, and marinated for an hour in the fridge.
7. Pre-heat your Blackstone griddle at 390°F and prepare your Blackstone for direct cooking.
8. Drain the skewers after marinating and set them immediately on the griddle.
9. Cook for around 8 mins, flipping the skewers on all sides.
10. Remove them out from the griddle as soon as they're done, place them on plates, and serve right away.

Nutrition:

Cal: 357, Fat 19g, Pro 15g, Carbs 9g

20. Sweet & Spicy Chicken Breasts

Prep: Fifteen min

Cook: Twenty min

Serves: 4

Ingredients:

- Two garlic cloves, minced
- extra-virgin olive oil ¼ cup
- low-sodium soy sauce ¼ cup
- One (1-inch) piece fresh ginger, minced
- One cup fresh pineapple juice
- One tsp ground cinnamon
- One tsp ground cumin
- 4 skinless, boneless chicken breasts
- Salt, as required

Directions:

1. In a plastic zippered bag, add chicken breast and remaining ingredients.

2. Seal the bag of chicken mixture tightly and shake to coat well.

3. Refrigerate to marinade for about 1 hour.

4. Pre-heat the Outdoor Gas Griddle to medium-high heat.

5. Grease the griddle. Generously

6. On the griddle, cook the chicken breasts for approximately 10 minutes on each side.

7. Serve hot.

Nutrition:

Cal 329, Pro 33.1 g, Fat 17.9 g, Carbs 10.2 g,

21. Grilled Tomahawk

Prep: Twenty min

Cook: Thirty min

Serves: 4

Ingredients:

- One sprig of rosemary
- Olive oil to taste
- Two cloves of garlic
- Two sage leaves
- Two tbsp of butter
- 4 juniper berries
- Two bay leaves
- 42 oz. of Tomahawk
- Salt & pepper to taste

Directions:

1. Bay leaves, rosemary, & sage should be washed and dried.
2. Garlic should be peeled and washed.
3. In a blender glass, combine the butter, garlic, fragrant herbs & juniper berries, oil, salt, & pepper.
4. Blend till the mixture is completely homogenous.
5. Remove all extra fat from the meat after washing and drying it.
6. On all sides, massage the meat using the flavored butter.
7. Pre-heat your Blackstone griddle at 350°F and prepare your Blackstone for the direct cooking.
8. Place the meat on the griddle & cook for around 10 mins.
9. Cook for another 5 mins perpendicularly before turning it over.
10. Carry out the same procedure on the other side.
11. The meat should be removed from the griddle and set aside to rest for 10 minutes on a chopping board.

12. Now chop the meat into slices & arrange them on serving dishes.

Nutrition:

Cal 540, Fat 20g, Pro 66g, Carbs 2g

22.   Citrusy Butter Pork Chops

Prep: Ten min

Cook: Thirty min

Serves: 4

Ingredients:

- 1 clove of garlic, minced
- 2 lemons, sliced into wedges
- 2 oranges, sliced into wedges
- 2 sticks of butter, softened
- 4 tbsp of fresh thyme leave, chopped
- 1 tsp of black pepper
- 5 pork chops
- 6 sprigs of rosemary, chopped

Directions:

1. Pre-heat your Blackstone griddle at medium temperature and apply a thin layer of oil on the griddle.
2. Squeeze the lemons and oranges onto a dish. Put together all the ingredients in a bowl, excluding the pork chops.
3. Marinate the pork chops for around 3 hours in the mixture. Cook for around 10 mins per side on the griddle.

Nutrition:

Cal 396, Fat 17g, Pro 32g, Carbs 7g

23.   Spicy Chicken Thighs

Prep: Ten min

Cook: Eighteen min

Serves: 8

Ingredients:

- garlic powder ½ tbsp
- One tbsp dried oregano, crushed
- One tbsp ground chipotle powder
- One tbsp paprika
- 2 tbsp fresh lime juice
- 8 (4-ounce) chicken thighs
- As required use Salt and ground black pepper

Directions:

1. The outdoor gas griddle should be Pre-heated to medium-high heat.
2. Give the griddle a lot of grease.
3. Except for the chicken thighs, combine all the ingredients in a dish with the lime juice.
4. Give the thighs a liberal coating of the spice mixture.
5. Cook the chicken thighs for about 8 minutes on the griddle.
6. Cook for an additional 8 to 10 minutes on the other side after carefully turning it over.
7. Serve hot.

Nutrition:

Cal 137, Fat 4.7 g, Carbs 1.3 g, Pro 22.4 g

24.   Grilled Beef Ribs

Prep: Ten min

Cook: Twenty min

Serves: 4

Ingredients:

- 2 sprigs of rosemary
- Salt & pepper to taste
- 4 beef ribs (5 oz. each)
- Olive oil to taste
- 1 clove of garlic

Directions:

1. The rosemary should be cleaned and dried before being chopped.
2. The garlic clove should be peeled & washed before being chopped.
3. Remove any excess fat out from the beef ribs by washing and drying them.
4. Season the ribs using oil, salt, rosemary, pepper, and garlic in a mixing bowl.
5. Refrigerate the bowl for 30 minutes to allow the ingredients to marinade.
6. Remove the meat from the fridge after 30 mins & set your Blackstone griddle for direct cooking at 390°F.
7. Cook the ribs for 3 mins on each side on the griddle.
8. Remove the meat out from the griddle after it has finished cooking and set it aside to rest for 5 mins.
9. Place the ribs onto serving dishes and serve after 5 mins.

Nutrition:

Cal 136, Fat 13g, Pro 24g, Carbs 2g

25.   Sweet & Sour Turkey Wings

Prep: Fifteen min

Cook: Forty-Four min

Serves: 6

Ingredients:

- red wine vinegar ¼ cup
- Two tbsp dark soy sauce
- 6 turkey wings
- 8 cups water
- 3 garlic cloves, chopped finely

- light brown sugar 1½ tbsp
- dried thyme ¾ tsp
- One tsp Tabasco sauce
- 2 scallions, chopped finely

Directions:

1. The turkey wings should be put in a pan with water and brought to a boil.
2. Boil for around 15 mins while the pan is covered with a lid.
3. Turn off the heat and put the turkey pan aside.
4. The outdoor gas griddle should be Pre-heated to medium to high heat.
5. All the remaining components for the sauce should be combined in a bowl.
6. Lightly grease the griddle.
7. Place the wings on the griddle after removing them from the water pan.

8. With a cooking dome, cover the wings and cook for about 12 mins.
9. After flipping them over, evenly coat the wings in sauce.
10. Cook the wings for 12 minutes with the cover on.
11. Again, flip the wings and coat with sauce evenly.
12. Cook for about 5 mins.
13. Transfer the wings onto a patter and coat with any remaining sauce.
14. Serve right away.

Nutrition:

Cal 611, Fat 37.8 g, Carbs 3.3 g, Pro 62.7 g

26.   Aromatic Vinegar Beef Tenderloin

Prep: Ten min

Cook: Twenty min

Serves: 4

Ingredients:

- Salt & pepper to taste
- 28 oz. of beef tenderloin
- Olive oil to taste
- 1 glass of balsamic vinegar

Directions:

1. Remove extra fat from the beef fillet by washing and drying it.
2. Season the beef using oil, salt, pepper, & balsamic vinegar in a mixing bowl.
3. To marinate, put cling film over the bowl and put it in the fridge for about two hours.
4. After the meat has had time to marinate, remove it from the refrigerator.
5. Pre-heat your Blackstone griddle at 390°F and prepare your Blackstone for the direct cooking.
6. Cook the beef on the griddle for around 20 mins, or till the internal temperature has reached 131°F.
7. Brush the meat using the marinade on a regular basis.
8. Remove the meat out from the griddle after it has finished cooking and set it aside to rest for 10 mins.
9. Cut the fillets into four slices after 10 mins.
10. Place the meat onto serving dishes and drizzle with the marinade before serving.

Nutrition:

Cal 337, Fat 10g, Pro 42g, Carbs 10g

Chapter 7.   Dinner

27.   Pork Sausages in White Wine

Prep: Ten min

Cook: Fifty min

Serves: 4

Ingredients:

- 2 glasses of white wine
- 8 pork sausages
- Olive oil to taste
- 2 cloves of garlic

Directions:

1. Pre-heat your Blackstone griddle at 280°F and prepare your Blackstone for indirect cooking.
2. Once the griddle has reached the desired temperature, evenly space the sausages on the griddle.
3. Cook for around 40 mins, turning them over every 5 mins with a little olive oil.
4. Place the wine in a baking dish in the meantime.
5. Garlic should be peeled and washed before being chopped and placed in the baking dish with wine.
6. Remove the sausages from the griddle after 40 mins and heat the wine.
7. Place the sausages in the baking dish once the mixture begins to boil.
8. Allow the sausages to rest for 15 mins after turning off the griddle.
9. Place the sausages on serving dishes after 15 mins.
10. Serve with a sprinkling of wine.

Nutrition:

Cal 809, Fat 32g, Pro 31g, Carbs 10g

28.   Grapefruit Marinated Beef Ribs

Prep: Ten min

Cook: Twenty min

Serves: 4

Ingredients:

- 8 mint leaves
- Olive oil to taste
- 4 beef cutlets (2 oz. each)
- 1 grapefruit
- 1 tbsp of pink pepper
- Salt & pepper to taste.

Directions:

1. Squeeze the grapefruit juice into the bowl and drain it.
2. Mint leaves should be washed and dried before being chopped.
3. In a bowl with grapefruit juice, combine the mint, salt, pink pepper, 4 tbsp of olive oil, and pepper.
4. Mix till you get a homogenous emulsion.
5. Remove any excess fat from the meat chops by washing and drying them.
6. The ribs should be put in the bowl with the marinade, covered with plastic wrap, and left to marinate for two hours.
7. Prepare your Blackstone griddle for direct cooking at 356°F at the end of the 2 hours.
8. Place the ribs on the griddle and cook for around 8 mins on each side, or till the meat reaches 140°F.
9. Turn the meat a few times and spray it with the marinade often.
10. Remove the ribs out from the griddle & set them aside for 10 mins to rest in the marinade.
11. Place the ribs on serving dishes and drizzle with a little marinade before serving.

Nutrition:

Cal 552, Fat 18g, Pro 52g, Carbs 6g

29.   Pork Loin Glazed with Honey

Prep: Fifteen min

Cook: Sixty min

Serves: 4

Ingredients:

- 2 sprigs of thyme
- 35 oz. of pork loin
- Salt & pepper to taste
- 2 sprigs of rosemary

- Olive oil to taste
- 4 sage leaves
- 1/2 cup of honey
- ½ glass of meat broth

Directions:

1. Mix the honey, beef broth, 5 tbsp olive oil, salt, and pepper in a bowl until they make a smooth emulsion.
2. Washing and drying the pork loin will get rid of any extra fat.
3. Pour the emulsion over the meat after placing it in a bowl.
4. Put cling film over the bowl and marinate for two hours in the refrigerator.
5. Pre-heat your griddle at 320°F and prepare your Blackstone for indirect cooking.
6. Place them on the griddle and place the loin on it.
7. Cook for 1 hour, or till the temperature of the meat reaches 167° F, with the probe in the center.
8. Every 10 mins, turn the meat and spray it using the marinade.
9. Remove the meat from the griddle after it has finished cooking and set it aside to rest for 10 mins.
10. Cut the meat into pieces and arrange on serving dishes after 10 mins.
11. Serve the marinade alongside the dish.

Nutrition:

Cal 334, Fat 10g, Pro 54g, Carbs 6g

30.   Pork Pineapple Skewers

Prep: Ten min

Cook: Fifteen min

Serves: 4

Ingredients:

- One lb. of pork fillet, cut into chunks
- One lime juice
- One tbsp of hot sauce
- One tsp of ground allspice
- Two cups of pineapple cubes
- Two tbsp of Creole seasoning

Directions:

1. Mix together the pork, pineapple cubes, hot sauce, lime juice, allspice, & spices in a mixing dish.
2. Pre-heat your griddle at medium-high.

3. Coat the top of the griddle using cooking spray.
4. Using skewers, thread pork & pineapple chunks.
5. Cook the skewers on a hot griddle till the pork is done.
6. Enjoy your meal.

Nutrition:

Cal 307, Fat 14g, Pro 32g, Carbs 11g

31. Dijon Pork Skewers

Prep: Ten min

Cook: Fifteen min

Serves: 4

Ingredients:

- Two cups cherry tomatoes
- Two cups bell peppers, cut into pieces
- Two cups mushrooms

For the marinade:

- ¼ cup of Dijon mustard
- ½ cup of vinaigrette

- 2 cups of onion, cut into pieces
- 1 ½ lbs. of pork loin, cut into 1-inch cubes

- Salt & ground black pepper

Directions:

1. Mix the pork cubes with the marinade ingredients in a mixing bowl & set aside for around 30 mins to marinate.
2. Using skewers, thread marinated pork cubes, onion, mushrooms, tomatoes, and bell peppers.
3. Pre-heat your griddle at medium-high.
4. Cook skewers for around 5-7 mins on each side or till cooked through on a hot griddle top.
5. Enjoy your meal.

Nutrition:

Cal 628, Fat 40g, Pro 50g, Carbs 16g

32.   Chicken & Avocado Burgers

Prep: Fifteen min

Cook: Ten min

Serves: 4

Ingredients:

- ½ cup Parmesan cheese, grated
- ½ of avocado, peeled, pitted and cut into chunks
- 1 garlic clove
- 1-pound lean ground chicken
- Salt
- ground black pepper

Directions:

1. Put the avocado chunks, Parmesan cheese, garlic, salt, and black pepper in a clean bowl and toss them all together.
2. Add the ground chicken to the avocado mixture in the bowl and stir it together gently.
3. Make 4 patties out of the chicken mixture. Each one should be the same size.
4. Pre-heat the Outdoor Gas Griddle to medium heat.
5. Grease the griddle generously.
6. Put the chicken patties on the griddle and cook them for about five mins on each side.
7. Serve right away.

Nutrition:

Cal 238, Fat 13.3 g, Carbs 2.4 g, Pro 27.5 g

33.   Chicken & Broccoli Kabobs

Prep: Fifteen min

Cook: Twenty min

Serves: 6

Ingredients:

- 1½ pounds skinless, boneless chicken breasts, cubed
- Two garlic cloves, minced
- Two tbsp dried marjoram, crushed
- Two tbsp olive oil
- Two tbsp tomato paste
- Four cups broccoli florets
- As required use Ground black pepper

Directions:

1. Mix the chicken, oil, marjoram, garlic, tomato paste, broccoli, and black pepper together well in a bowl.
2. Cover the bowl of chicken mixture and let it sit at room temperature for about 10–15 minutes.
3. Pre-heat the Outdoor Gas Griddle to medium heat.
4. Thread the chicken and broccoli onto pre-soaked wooden skewers.
5. Grease the griddle generously.
6. Place the chicken skewers on the griddle and cook for about 8 to 10 minutes per side, or until the chicken is as done as you like it.
7. Serve hot.

Nutrition:

Cal: 210, Fat 9 g, Carbs 5.7 g, Pro 27.4 g

34.   Grilled Steaks with Potatoes

Prep: Fifteen min

Cook: Twenty min

Serves: 4

Ingredients:

- 10.5 oz. of potatoes
- 4 beef steaks (7 oz. each)
- Salt & pepper to taste
-

- 2 sprigs of rosemary
- Olive oil to taste

Directions:

1. Let's begin with the potatoes. They should be peeled, washed, and then cut into wedges.
2. Drain the potatoes after boiling them in salted water.
3. Put the potatoes in the baking pan and brush them with olive oil.
4. The rosemary should be washed and dried before being placed in the baking pan with potatoes.
5. Pre-heat your Blackstone griddle at 390°F and prepare your Blackstone for the direct/indirect cooking.
6. Cook for 15 mins on indirect heat in the pan with the potatoes.
7. Remove any excess fat from the steaks by washing and drying them.
8. After you've brushed them with olive oil, season them with salt and pepper.
9. Put the steaks directly over the heat.
10. Cook for another 6 mins before flipping the steaks.
11. Continue cooking for another 6 mins, or till the meat reaches a core temperature of 131°F.
12. Remove the meat & potatoes from the griddle once they've finished cooking.
13. Place the steaks on the plates, top with the potatoes, & serve.

Nutrition:

Cal 362, Fat 13g, Pro 45g, Carbs 15g

35. Beefsteak in Red Wine

Prep: Fifteen min

Cook: Fifteen min

Serves: 4

Ingredients:

- 1 bottle of red wine
- Salt & pepper to taste
- 4 beef steaks (10.5 oz. each)
- Two sprigs of rosemary
- Olive oil to taste

Directions:

1. To begin, wash the steak and blot it dry using a paper towel.
2. Salt and black pepper, along with a little olive oil, are used to season the steaks.
3. Rinse & dry the rosemary leaves.
4. Now pour the red wine into a resalable bag.
5. Close the bag and add the steaks and rosemary.
6. Let the steaks marinate in the fridge for at least two hours.
7. Take out the meat from the fridge after two hours.
8. Pre-heat your Blackstone griddle at 400°F and prepare your Blackstone griddle for the direct cooking.
9. Remove the steaks from the red wine marinade.
10. Cook the meat steaks over direct fire.
11. Cook for around 10 mins, or till the beef reaches a core temperature of 131° F, flipping occasionally.
12. Take out the steaks from the griddle and set them aside for around 10 mins to rest.
13. Remove the bone out from the steaks & chop them into strips before serving.
14. Add a sprinkle of oil, salt, and pepper before serving.

Nutrition:

Cal 812, Fat 25g, Pro 64g, Carbs 5g

36. Pork Fillet with Fennel Seeds

Prep: Fifteen min

Cook: Thirty-Five min

Serves: 4

Ingredients:

- Olive oil to taste
- 21 oz. of pork tenderloin
- Salt and pepper to taste
- Three tbsp fennel seeds

Directions:

1. Remove the excess fat out from the pork tenderloin by washing and drying it.
2. Brush the fillet using olive oil, then season with salt, pepper, & fennel seeds all over.
3. Tie the fillet using kitchen string to keep it from deforming during the cooking process.
4. Pre-heat your griddle at 320°F and prepare your Blackstone for indirect cooking.
5. Place the fillet on the griddle and cook for around 35 mins, or till the internal temperature reaches 154°F.
6. Take out the meat from the griddle after it has finished cooking and set it aside to rest for 10 mins.
7. Remove the kitchen thread after 10 mins and slice them into slices.
8. Serve the meat on serving platters.

Nutrition:

Cal 204, Fat 13g, Pro 32g, Carbs 2g

37.   Beef Sirloin with Aromatic Herbs

Prep: Fifteen min

Cook: Twenty min

Serves: 4

Ingredients:

- 4 sprigs of rosemary
- 28 oz. of beef sirloin
- Olive oil to taste
- 4 sprigs of marjoram
- 4 sprigs of thyme
- Salt & pepper to taste
- 4 sage leaves

Directions:

1. Remove extra fat from the sirloin by washing and drying it.

2. Thyme, marjoram, sage, and rosemary should be washed and dried before being chopped as fine as possible.
3. Mix the herbs, salt, pepper, and 4 tbsp olive oil in a bowl.
4. Brush the meat using the herb mixture after it has been thoroughly mixed.
5. Pre-heat your Blackstone griddle at 400°F and prepare your Blackstone for the direct cooking.
6. Place the meat on the griddle & cook for around 16 mins, or till it reaches a temperature of 131°F.
7. Brush the meat with the herb marinade regularly.
8. Remove the meat out from the griddle after it has finished cooking and set it aside to rest for 10 mins.
9. Put the meat on a cutting board and cut it into pieces.
10. Serve the meat on serving dishes, seasoned with a little herb marinade.

Nutrition:

Cal 348, Fat 16g, Pro 52g, Carbs 2g

38.   Flank Steak with Garlic and Rosemary

Prep: Ten min

Cook: Twenty min

Serves: 4

Ingredients:

- 2 (8 ounces) of flank steaks

For the marinade:

- One tbsp of extra virgin olive oil, plus more for brushing
- black pepper 1/4 tsp
- Two tbsp of fresh rosemary, chopped
- Two tsp of sea salt
- 4 cloves of garlic, minced

Directions:

1. Pulse the marinade ingredients in a food processor or blender until the garlic and rosemary are crushed.
2. Prick the steaks Ten times on each side using a fork.
3. On both sides, rub each using the marinade evenly.
4. Refrigerate it for at least 1 hour or overnight in a covered dish.
5. Pre-heat your Blackstone griddle at medium-high temperature and apply a thin layer of oil on the griddle.

6. Cook for around 5 mins on one side, then flip, tent using foil, & cook for another 3-4 mins.
7. Put the meat on a cutting board and cover it with aluminum foil so that it can rest for 15 minutes.
8. Serve immediately after slicing very thinly against the grain.

Nutrition:

Cal 260, Fat 13g, Pro 41g, Carbs 4g

39.   Chipotle Turkey Burger

Prep: Fifteen min

Cook: Ten min

Serves: 4

Ingredients:

- One pound extra lean ground turkey
- One garlic clove, minced
- One tbsp chili powder
- As required use Salt and ground black pepper
- 2-2¼ tbsp chipotle chili in adobo sauce, pureed

Directions:

1. Mix the ground turkey and the rest of the ingredients together in a bowl until everything is well mixed.
2. Refrigerate for about 6-8 hours.
3. Pre-heat the Outdoor Gas Griddle to medium-high heat.
4. Make 4 equal-sized patties from the mixture.
5. Make a small hole in the middle of each one with your thumb.
6. Grease the griddle thoroughly.
7. Put the patties onto the griddle, dent side down and cook about 5 mins per side.
8. Serve hot.

Nutrition:

Cal 180, Fat 8.4 g, Carbs 1. 5 g, Pro 21.6 g

40.   Thyme Duck Breast

Prep: Ten min

Cook: Sixteen min

Serves: 4

Ingredients:

- Two shallots, sliced thinly
- Two tbsp chopped fresh thyme
- As required use Salt and ground black pepper
- 4 duck breasts

Directions:

1. Mix shallots, thyme, salt, and black pepper in a clean bowl.
2. Make small cuts in the skin of the breast in a crosshatch pattern with a sharp knife, as shown.
3. Rub the duck breasts generously with thyme mixture.
4. Cover the bowl of duck breasts and put it in the fridge for about 12 hours so that it can marinate.
5. Pre-heat the Outdoor Gas Griddle to medium-high heat.
6. Grease the griddle generously.
7. Put the duck breasts onto the griddle, skin side down and cook for about 6-8 mins per side.
8. Remove from griddle and place the duck breasts onto a platter for about 5 mins before slicing.
9. With a sharp knife, cut each duck breast into desired sized slices and serve.

Nutrition:

Cal 376, Fat 11.5 g, Carbs 2.5 g, Pro 62.7 g

41. Caprese Flank Steak

Prep: Ten min

Cook: Fifteen min

Serves: 4

Ingredients:

- 2 Roma tomatoes, sliced
- Sea salt for seasoning
- 4 (6 ounces) of flank steaks
- 8 fresh basil leaves
- Fresh ground pepper
- Balsamic vinegar glaze for drizzling
- Flakey sea salt, for serving
- Olive oil
- 4 ounces of fresh buffalo mozzarella, cut into four slices

Directions:

1. Put olive oil on all sides of each fillet and season with salt and pepper.
2. Set your Blackstone griddle to medium-high heat and spread a thin layer of oil over it. Cook the steaks for about 5 minutes on the griddle.
3. Cook for an additional 5 mins after flipping, re-tenting, and topping each with a piece of mozzarella during the last two mins of cooking.
4. Take the steaks off the griddle and place a few tomato slices and two basil leaves on each one before serving.
5. Drizzle with the balsamic glaze and season with flaky salt and pepper to taste.

Nutrition:

Cal 461, Fat 23g, Pro 56g, Carbs 6g

Chapter 8.   Snacks

42.   Corn Cakes

Prep: Ten min

Cook: Ten min

Serves: 10

Ingredients:

- One jalapeno, chopped
- cheddar cheese 1/2 cup, shredded
- Cornmeal 1/2 cup
- flour 1/2 cup
- kosher salt 1/2 tsp
- pepper 1/2 tsp
- Two cups corn
- green onions 2/3 cup, sliced
- Four eggs

Directions:

1. Put the corn in the food processor and pulse it until it looks like small pieces.
2. Add the corn and the remaining ingredients to the bowl and mix until everything is well combined.
3. Pre-heat the griddle to high heat.
4. Spray cooking spray on the top of the griddle.
5. Make patties out of the mixture and place them on a hot griddle top. Cook until both sides are light golden brown.
6. Serve and relish.

Nutrition:

Cal: 122; Fat: 4.3 g; Carbs: 16.1 g; Pro: 5.9 g

43.
Quick Cheese Toast

Prep: Ten min

Cook: Eight min

Serves: 4

Ingredients:

- One cup bell pepper, chopped
- One cup mozzarella cheese, shredded
- Two green chilies, chopped
- Four garlic cloves, minced
- Eight bread slices
- Pepper and Salt

Directions:

1. Mix bell pepper, green chili, and garlic and spread evenly over bread slices. Top with cheese, pepper, and salt.
2. Pre-heat the griddle to medium heat.
3. Spray griddle top with cooking spray.
4. Place bread slices on hot griddle top cover and cook until cheese melts.
5. Serve and relish.

Nutrition:

Cal: 87; Fat: 1.9 g; Carbs: 13.6 g; Pro: 3.9 g

44. Chickpea Burger Patties

Prep: Ten min

Cook: Twelve min

Serves: 6

Ingredients:

- Three eggs
- Two cups cauliflower florets
- One tsp garlic powder
- Two tbsp parsley, chopped
- Pepper and Salt
- onion powder 1/2 tsp
- onion 1/2 cup, chopped
- 1 ¾ cups can chickpeas, drained

Directions:

1. Put the florets of cauliflower and chickpeas in the food processor and chop them up until they are small.
2. Add the remaining ingredients and process until everything is just mixed.
3. Pre-heat the griddle to medium heat.

4. Make patties from mixture and place on hot griddle top and cook until lightly browned from both sides.
5. Serve and relish.

Nutrition:

Cal: 130; Fat: 3 g; Carbs: 19.3 g; Pro: 7.2 g

45.   Easy Pineapple Slices

Prep: Ten min

Cook: Twelve min

Serves: 4

Ingredients:

- Four pineapple slices
- One tbsp butter, melted
- chili powder ¼ tsp
- Salt

Directions:

1. Pre-heat the griddle to high heat.
2. Brush pineapple slices with butter, chili powder, and salt.
3. Place pineapple slices on a hot griddle top and cook for 5–6 mins on each side.
4. Serve and relish.

Nutrition:

Cal: 108; Fat: 3.1 g; Carbs: 21.7 g; Pro: 0.9 g

46.   Coconut Chocolate Simple Brownies

Prep: Fifteen min

Cook: Twenty-Five min

Serves: 6

Ingredients:

- 4 eggs
- 1 cup Cane Sugar
- ¾ cup Coconut oil
- 4 ounces chocolate, chopped
- ½ tsp Sea salt
- ¼ cup cocoa powder, unsweetened
- ½ cup flour
- 4 ounces Chocolate chips
- One tsp Vanilla

Directions:

1. Pre-heat the griddle to 350°F with the lid closed.
2. Take a baking pan (9x9), grease it, and line a parchment paper.
3. Combine the flour, cocoa powder, and salt in a bowl. Stir, then put aside.
4. Melt the coconut oil and chopped chocolate in a double boiler or microwave. Let it rest for a while.
5. Add the sugar, eggs, and vanilla. Combine by whisking.
6. Add the chocolate chunks to the flour. In a pan, pour the ingredients.
7. On the grate, set the pan. For 20 minutes, bake. Bake the brownies for 5–10 minutes longer if you want them dryer.
8. Let them cool before cutting.
9. Cut the brownies into squares and serve.

Nutrition:

Cal: 135; Pro: 2 g; Carbs: 16 g; Fat: 3 g

47.   Cajun Turkey Club

Prep: Five min

Cook: Ten min

Serves: 3

Ingredients:

- 1 3 lb. Turkey Breast
- 1 Butter stick (melted)
- 8 ounces Chicken Broth
- 1 tbsp Killer Hogs Hot Sauce
- 1/4 cup Malcolm's King Craw Seasoning
- 8 Pieces to Thick Sliced Bacon
- 1 head Green Leaf Lettuce
- 1 Tomato (sliced)
- 6 slices Toasted Bread
- ½ cup Cajun Mayo
- One cup mayo
- One tbsp Dijon Mustard
- One tbsp Killer Hogs Sweet Fire Pickles (chopped)
- One tbsp Horseradish
- 1 cup Brown Sugar
- ½ tsp Malcolm's King Craw Seasoning
- 1 tsp Killer Hogs Hot Sauce
- A pinch Salt & Black Pepper to taste

Directions:

1. Pre-heat the griddle 325°F
2. In a blender, combine the margarine that has been dissolved with the chicken stock, spicy sauce, and 1 tbsp of Cajun seasoning. Spread the infusion spots out to ensure even inclusion when you infuse the mixture into the turkey's bosom.
3. Shower the outside of the turkey bosom with a Vegetable cooking splash and season with Malcolm's King Craw Seasoning.
4. The turkey breast should be placed on the griddle and cooked until the internal temperature reaches 165°F. Use a moment-read thermometer to monitor the temperature during cooking.
5. Consolidate darker sugar and 1 tsp of King Craw in a little bowl. Spread the bacon with the sugar blend and place it on a cooling rack.
6. Cook the bacon for 12 to 15 mins or until darker. Make certain to turn the bacon part of the way through for cooking.
7. Toast the bread, cut the tomatoes dainty, and wash/dry the lettuce leaves.
8. At the point when the turkey bosom arrives at 165°F take it from the flame broil and rest for 15 mins. Take the netting out from around the bosom and cut it into slender cuts.
9. To cause the sandwich: To slather Cajun Mayo* on the toast, stack on a few cuts of turkey bosom, lettuce, tomato, and bacon. Include another bit of toast and rehash a similar procedure. Include the top bit of toast slathered with more Cajun mayo, cut the sandwich into equal parts and appreciate.

Nutrition:

Cal: 130; Carbs: 1 g; Fat: 4 g; Pro: 21 g

48.   Bacon Chocolate Chip Cookies

Prep: Thirty min

Cook: Thirty min

Serves: 6

Ingredients:

- 8 slices cooked and crumbled bacon
- Two room temp eggs
- Two cup semisweet chocolate chips
- All-purpose flour 2 ¾ cup
- apple cider vinegar 2 ½ tsp

- One tsp vanilla
- One cup light brown sugar
- One cup granulated sugar
- baking soda 1 ½ tsp
- stick softened butter 1 ½
- salt ½ tsp

Directions:

1. Mix salt, baking soda, and flour.
2. Cream the sugar and the butter together. Lower the speed. Add in the eggs, vinegar, and vanilla.
3. Put it on low fire, slowly add in the flour mixture, bacon pieces, and chocolate chips.
4. Pre-heat your griddle, with your lid closed, until it reaches 375°F.
5. Put parchment paper on the baking sheet you are using and drop a teaspoon of cookie dough on it. Let them cook on the griddle, covered, for approximately 12 mins or until they are browned.

Nutrition:

Cal: 167; Carbs: 21 g; Fat: 9 g; Pro: 2 g

49.   Tasty Bread Pizza

Prep: Ten min

Cook: Ten min

Serves: 4

Ingredients:

- 4 bread slices

For toppings:

- Two tbsp pizza sauce
- Ten olives, sliced
- red chili flakes 1/4 tsp
- oregano 1/2 tsp

- mozzarella cheese 1/2 cup, grated
- bell pepper 1/2 cup, cubed
- One small tomato, cubed
- One onion, cubed

Directions:

1. Spread pizza sauce on bread slices. Top with olives, tomatoes, bell pepper, and onion.
2. Sprinkle with chili flakes, oregano, and cheese.
3. Pre-heat the griddle to medium heat.
4. Put the bread slices on the hot top of the griddle, cover it, and cook until the cheese melts.
5. Serve and relish.

Nutrition:

Cal: 71; Fat: 2.3 g; Carbs: 11 g; Pro: 2.6 g

50.   Veggie Patties

Prep: Ten min

Cook: Ten min

Serves: 6

Ingredients:

- One cup breadcrumbs
- One cup carrots, shredded
- One cup potatoes, shredded
- One cup zucchini, shredded

- 1/2 cup onion, chopped
- 2 eggs
- 2 tbsp parsley, chopped
- Pepper and Salt

Directions:

1. Put all of the ingredients in the bowl and mix them together well.

2. Pre-heat the griddle to high heat.
3. Spray griddle top with cooking spray.
4. Make patties from mixture and place on hot griddle top and cook until lightly golden brown from both sides.
5. Serve and relish.

Nutrition:

Cal: 124; Fat: 2.5 g; Carbs: 20.4 g; Pro: 5.2 g

51. Tomato Avocado Bruschetta

Prep: Ten min

Cook: Ten min

Serves: 6

Ingredients:

- 6 bread slices
- 2 tbsp olive oil

For topping:

- One avocado, peel & dice
- One cucumber, diced
- One garlic clove, minced
- One tomato, chopped
- Sea salt 1/4 tsp

Directions:

1. Pre-heat the griddle to high heat.
2. Spread oil on bread slices and place them on a hot griddle top. Cook until both sides are light golden brown.
3. Put all of the topping ingredients in a bowl and mix them well.
4. Spoon topping mixture over bread slices.
5. Serve and relish.

Nutrition:

Cal: 142; Fat: 11.6 g; Carbs: 9.8 g; Pro: 1.8 g

Chapter 9.   Side Dish

52.   Cheesy Corn

Prep: Fifteen min

Cook: Twenty-Two min

Serves: 6

Ingredients:

- 4 bacon slices
- 3 cups frozen corn, thawed
- 1 tsp chili margarita seasoning
- ½ tsp fresh cracked pepper
- 2 ounces cream cheese, softened
- ¼ cup whole milk
- ½ cup cotija cheese
- Three tbsp scallions, chopped
- Two tbsp fresh cilantro, chopped

Directions:

1. Pre-heat the Outdoor Gas Griddle to medium-low heat.
2. Arrange the bacon slices onto the griddle in a single layer and cook for about 10-12 mins or until it is crisp.
3. Remove the bacon, leaving the grease onto the griddle.
4. Place the bacon onto a paper towel-lined plate t0 drain.
5. Then cut the bacon into small pieces.
6. Put the corn on the griddle and stir it often while cooking for about 2 to 3 minutes.
7. Mix in the seasoning for margaritas and the black pepper. Toss to combine.
8. With a wooden spoon, create a well in the middle of the corn pile.
9. Place the cream cheese and milk in the well and cook for about 1-2 mins.
10. Then stir the cream cheese mixture with corn.
11. Add the chopped bacon, cotija cheese and scallion and stir to combine.
12. With a cooking dome, cover the corn mixture and cook for about 1-2 mins.
13. Garnish with cilantro and serve hot.

Nutrition:

Cal 243, Fat 15.2 g, Carbs 16 g, Pro 12.8 g

53.   Smashed Potatoes

Prep: Fifteen min

Cook: Seven min

Serves: 6

Ingredients:

- ¼ tsp granulated garlic
- One tbsp fresh parsley, chopped
- 1/3 cup Parmesan cheese, shredded
- 2 pounds small Yukon gold potatoes
- 3 tbsp butter, melted
- 4 tbsp vegetable oil, divided
- Salt and ground black pepper, as required

Directions:

1. Pre-heat the Outdoor Gas Griddle to medium-low heat.
2. Arrange the potatoes onto a metal sheet tray and drizzle with 2 tbsp of olive oil.
3. With a potato masher, smash each potato lightly into ¼-½ inch thickness.
4. Mix the butter and garlic powder together in a small, clean bowl.
5. Sprinkle salt and black pepper on each potato after brushing it with the butter mixture.
6. Place the remaining oil on the griddle.
7. Add the potatoes that have been flattened, and cook for about 3 minutes.
8. Flip the potatoes and sprinkle with half of Parmesan cheese.
9. Cook for about 3 mins.
10. Flip the potatoes and sprinkle with remaining Parmesan cheese.
11. Cook for about one minute.
12. Serve warm, with the garnishing of parsley.

Nutrition:

Cal 193, Fat 15.1 g, Carbs 0.4 g, Pro 3 g

54.   Red Chili Broccolini

Prep: Fifteen min

Cook: Four min

Serves: 2

Ingredients:

- One medium red chili, thinly sliced
- One tbsp sesame oil
- Two tbsp balsamic vinegar
- Two tbsp olive oil
- Two tbsp soy sauce
- 3 tbsp fresh chervil, chopped
- 8 ounces broccolini

Directions:

1. Pre-heat the Outdoor Gas Griddle to medium-high heat.
2. Brush the broccoli lightly with the olive oil.
3. Grease the griddle.
4. Add the broccolini to the griddle and cook for about 3-4 mins, flipping occasionally.
5. Meanwhile, mix together the remaining ingredients into a bowl.
6. Place the broccolini onto a serving plate.
7. Drizzle with chili mixture and serve.

Nutrition:

Cal 237, Fat 20.9 g, Carbs 10.3 g, Pro 4.9 g

55.   Parmesan Asparagus

Prep: Fifteen min

Cook: Thirty-Five min

Serves: 4

Ingredients:

- ½ cup heavy cream
- One cup balsamic vinegar

- One tbsp fresh lemon juice
- One tsp salt
- 1-pound fresh asparagus, tough ends removed
- 2 tbsp vegetable oil
- 3 tbsp Parmesan cheese, grated and divided

Directions:

1. For balsamic reduction, put balsamic vinegar in a small pan and bring it to a boil over high heat.
2. Turn down the heat and let it cook for about 20 minutes.
3. Pre-heat the Outdoor Gas Griddle to medium heat.
4. For the Parmesan sauce, put the heavy cream and 2 tablespoons of Parmesan cheese in a small pan over low heat and stir often for about 10 to 12 minutes.
5. Put the asparagus, oil, and salt in a bowl and toss well to coat.
6. Grease the griddle.
7. Place the asparagus onto the griddle and cook for about 10 mins, flipping occasionally.
8. Pour some lemon juice over the cooked asparagus in a bowl.
9. Spread the balsamic reduction over the asparagus on serving plates.
10. Garnish with remaining Parmesan cheese and serve alongside the sauce.

Nutrition:

Cal 193, Fat 15.5 g, Carbs 6.2 g, Pro 7.3 g

56.   Parmesan Broccoli

Prep: One min

Cook: Nine min

Serves: 6

Ingredients:

- 2 pounds broccoli florets
- 2 tbsp olive oil
- As required use Salt and ground black pepper
- ½ cup Parmesan cheese, shredded

Directions:

1. Put the Outdoor Gas Griddle on medium-high heat to get it ready.
2. Put a little bit of salt in some water in a pot and bring it to a boil over medium-high heat.
3. After the water has come to a boil, add the broccoli florets and cook for about 3 minutes.
4. After well-draining the broccoli, put it right into a bowl of iced water.
5. Drain the broccoli once more and pat it dry with a paper towel.
6. Lightly brush the broccoli with olive oil and add salt and black pepper to taste.
7. Grease the griddle lightly.
8. Put the broccoli florets on the griddle and cook them for about three to four minutes.
9. Flip the broccoli and cook for another minute or two.
10. Serve right away with a sprinkle of Parmesan cheese on top.

Nutrition:

Cal 118, Fat 7 g, Carbs 10.3 g, Pro 6.8 g

57. Herbed Eggplant

Prep: Fifteen min

Cook: Six min

Serves: 4

Ingredients:

- ½ cup extra-virgin olive oil
- Two eggplants, cut into ¼-inch thick slices
- Two tbsp fresh oregano, chopped
- Two tbsp fresh parsley, chopped
- Three garlic cloves, crushed
- Ground black pepper, as required
- Salt, as required

Directions:

1. Set the gas griddle outside to medium heat.
2. Place the eggplant slices in a strainer and sprinkle them with a lot of salt.
3. Set aside for about 15 mins.
4. With a paper towel, wipe each eggplant slice to remove the salt and moisture.
5. In a bowl, mix olive oil, herbs, garlic, salt, and black pepper together with a whisk.

6. Put the eggplant slices in the bowl with the oil mixture and toss to coat.

7. Grease the griddle generously.

6. Cook the eggplant slices for about 6 minutes per side on the griddle.

7. Serve hot.

Nutrition:

Cal 295, Fat 26 g, Carbs 18.4 g, Pro 3.1 g

58.   Sweet & Sour Carrots

Prep: Ten min

Cook: Twelve min

Serves: 6

Ingredients:

- ½ tsp garlic powder
- One tsp dried oregano, crushed
- One tsp ground cumin
- 1½ pounds small carrots, peeled and halved lengthwise
- Two tbsp honey
- Three tbsp olive oil
- Three tsp balsamic vinegar
- Salt and ground black pepper, as required

Directions:

1. Blend together all ingredients, except for carrots, into a bowl.
2. Add the carrots and toss to coat well.
3. Set aside, covered for about 1½ hours.
4. Pre-heat the Outdoor Gas Griddle to medium heat.
5. Grease the griddle.
6. Place the carrot slices onto the griddle in a single layer and cover with a cooking dome.
7. Cook for about 8-12 mins, flipping occasionally.
8. Serve hot.

Nutrition:

Cal 131, Fat 7.1 g, Carbs 17.4 g, Pro 1.1 g

59. Lemony Summer Squash

Prep: Ten min

Cook: Twelve min

Serves: 4

Ingredients:

- One tbsp fresh lemon juice
- One tsp dried rosemary, crushed
- 1-pound yellow squash, cut into ½-inch slices
- Two tbsp canola oil
- Salt and ground black pepper, as required

Directions:

1. Pre-heat the Outdoor Gas Griddle to medium heat.
2. Blend together all ingredients except for carrots into a bowl.
3. Add the squash slices and toss to coat well.
4. Grease the griddle.
5. Place the squash slices onto the griddle in a single layer and cover with a cooking dome.
6. Cook for about 10-12 mins, flipping occasionally.
7. Serve hot.

Nutrition:

Cal 82, Fat 7.3 g, Carbs 4.1 g, Pro 1.4 g

60. Spiced Cauliflower

Prep: Ten min

Cook: Fifteen min

Serves: 2

Ingredients:

- garlic powder ¼ tsp
- onion powder ¼ tsp

- paprika ½ tsp
- Two cups fresh cauliflower florets
- As required use Salt and ground black pepper

Directions:

1. Pre-heat the Outdoor Gas Griddle to medium heat.
2. Mix everything together in a bowl.
3. Put the cauliflower florets on heavy-duty foil that is double thick.
4. To seal the cauliflower florets, fold the foil around them.
5. Place the foil packet onto the griddle and cook for about 10-15 mins.
6. Serve hot.

Nutrition:

Cal 29, Fat 0.2 g, Carbs 6.1 g, Pro 2.2 g

61. Green Beans with Cranberries

Prep: Ten min

Cook: Ten min

Serves: 4

Ingredients:

- One tsp fresh lemon juice
- One tsp sesame seeds
- 1/3 cup dried cranberries
- 1-pound fresh green beans, trimmed
- Two garlic cloves, chopped
- 2-3 tbsp water
- Three tbsp unsalted butter
- Salt and ground black pepper, as required

Directions:

1. Pre-heat the Outdoor Gas Griddle to medium heat.
2. On the griddle, put the butter and let it melt.
3. Salt and black pepper the green beans, then add them to the pan and cook for about 3 to 4 mins, stirring often.
4. Stir the garlic and cranberries together after you add them.

5. Add some water and let the beans cook for about 3–5 minutes, or until they are soft.
6. Pour the cooked green beans and the rest of the ingredients into a bowl and drizzle with lemon juice.
7. Serve hot and sprinkle with sesame seeds.

Nutrition:

Cal 123, Fat 9.2 g, Carbs 9.6 g, Pro 2.4 g

Chapter 10. Seafood

62.   Spiced Snapper with Mango and Red Onion Salad

Prep: Five min

Cook: Twenty-Five min

Serves: 3

Ingredients:

- 2 red snappers, cleaned
- Sea salt
- 1/3 cup tandoori spice

For the salsa:

- 1 bunch cilantro, coarsely chopped
- 1 ripe but firm mango, peeled and chopped

- Olive oil, plus more for the grill
- Extra-virgin olive oil for drizzling
- Lime wedges, for serving

- One small red onion, thinly sliced
- Three tbsp fresh lime juice

Directions:

1. Mix the mango, onion, cilantro, lime juice, a big pinch of salt, and a bit of olive oil in a medium bowl. Toss again to coat.
2. Put the snapper on a cutting board and use paper towels to dry it. With a sharp knife, cut diagonal cuts across the body every 2 inches on both sides, all the way down to the bones.
3. Salt the fish well on the outside and inside. Spice the fish with tandoori.
4. Oil the griddle and heat it over medium-high heat.
5. Grill the fish for 10 minutes without moving it, until the skin is puffed up and blackened.
6. About 8 to 12 minutes later, flip the fish and grill it until the other side is lightly charred and the skin is puffed up.
7. Move to a serving platter.
8. Serve with lime wedges and mango salad on top.

Nutrition:

Cal: 211 Fat: 5.4 g Carbs: 18.9 g Pro: 23.6 g

63.   Honey-Lime Tilapia and Corn Foil Pack

Prep: Five min

Cook: Fifteen Min

Serves: 4

Ingredients:

- 1/4 cup olive oil
- Two ears corn, shucked
- Two tbsp fresh cilantro leaves
- Two tbsp honey

- 4 fillets tilapia
- 4 limes, thinly sliced
- Freshly ground black pepper
- Kosher salt

Directions:

1. Pre-heat griddle to high.
2. Cut four 12" squares out of the foil.
3. Place a piece of tilapia on top of each piece of foil.
4. Honey, lime, corn, and cilantro go on top of the tilapia.
5. Add some olive oil and sea salt and pepper to taste.
6. Cook for about 15 minutes, or until the tilapia is fully cooked and the corn is tender.

Nutrition:

Cal: 319 Fat: 14.7 g Carbs: 30.3 g Pro: 24 g

64.   Mexican Shrimp Tacos

Prep: Fifteen Min

Cook: Twelve min

Serves: 5

Ingredients:

- 2 lbs. medium shrimp, peeled and deveined
- 8 flour tortillas, warmed

For marinade:

- One bag cabbage slaw
- One cup salsa
- One cup Mexican crema

- One tbsp chili powder
- One tbsp cumin
- One tbsp fresh lime juice
- One tbsp garlic powder
- 1/4 tsp sea salt
- 1/8 tsp fresh ground pepper
- Two tbsp olive oil

Directions:

1. Pre-heat a griddle to medium-high.
2. Mix oil marinade in a large plastic bag that can be sealed. Add the shrimp and toss to coat. Let the shrimp marinate for 30 minutes in the fridge.
3. Cook shrimp for three minutes on each side, or until they are fully cooked.
4. Move onto a plate.
5. Lay two tortillas on each plate. Evenly divide the shrimp, cabbage slaw, salsa in the middle of each tortilla.
6. Drizzle with Mexican crema and serve.

Nutrition:

Cal: 400 Fat: 14.7 g Carbs: 30.3 g Pro: 24 g

65.   Bacon Wrapped Scallops

Prep: Five min

Cook: Two Min

Serves: 3

Ingredients:

- 12 large sea scallops, side muscle removed
- 8 slices of bacon
- 1 tbsp vegetable oil
- 12 toothpicks

Directions:

1. Set your griddle to medium heat and cook the bacon until the fat has rendered but the bacon is still bendable. Put the bacon on paper towels after taking it off the griddle.
2. Raise the heat on the griddle to medium-high.
3. Wrap half a slice of bacon around each scallop and use a toothpick to keep the bacon in place.
4. Place the scallops on the griddle and cook for 90 seconds per side. They should be lightly browned on both sides.
5. Remove from the griddle and serve immediately.

Nutrition:

Cal: 315 Fat: 20 g Carbs: 2.7 g Pro: 29.2 g

66. Scallops with Lemony Salsa Verde

Prep: Fifteen Min

Cook: Two Min

Serves: 3

Ingredients:

- 1 tbsp olive oil, plus more for grilling
- 12 large sea scallops, side muscle removed
- Sea salt, for seasoning

For the Lemony Salsa Verde:

- One garlic clove, finely chopped
- One small shallot, finely chopped
- 1/2 cup finely chopped fresh cilantro
- 1/2 lemon, with peel, seeded and chopped
- 1/4 cup chopped fresh chives
- olive oil 1/4 cup
- black pepper 1/4 tsp
- sea salt 1/4 tsp
- 3/4 cup finely chopped fresh parsley
- 5 tomatillos, peeled and pulsed in a blender

Directions:

1. Toss Lemony Salsa ingredients in a small mixing bowl and set aside.
2. Pre-heat griddle for medium-high and brush with olive oil.
3. Toss scallops with 1 tbsp olive oil on a baking sheet and season with salt.
4. Add scallops to the griddle, turning once after 45 seconds to 1 minute. Cook an additional 1 minute before removing from the griddle.
5. Serve scallops topped with Lemony Salsa Verde.

Nutrition:

Cal: 267 Fat: 9.6 g Carbs: 13.9 g Pro: 32.4 g

67. Grilled Oysters with Spiced Tequila Butter

Prep: Five min

Cook: Three Min

Serves: 6

Ingredients:

- 3 dozen medium oysters, scrubbed and shucked

For the butter:

- 1 tsp dried oregano
- 1/4 tsp chili oil
- 1/4 tsp crushed red pepper

- Flakey sea salt, for serving

- 2 tbsp freshly squeezed lemon juice
- 2 tbsp Tequila Blanco, like Espolon
- 7 tbsp unsalted butter

Directions:

1. Combine butter ingredients in a small mixing bowl until well incorporated and set aside.
2. Pre-heat griddle to high.
3. Grill the oysters for about 1 to 2 mins.
4. Sprinkle the oysters with salt flakes.
5. Warm the butter in a microwave for 60 seconds, and spoon the warm Tequila butter over the oysters and serve.

Nutrition:

Cal: 184 Fat: 15 g Carbs: 3.8 g Pro: 0.2 g

68.   Halibut Fillets with Spinach and Olives

Prep: Five min

Cook: Eleven Min

Serves: 4

Ingredients:

- 4 (6 ounces) halibut fillets
- 4 cups baby spinach

- 2 ounces pitted black olives, halved
- 2 tbsp flat-leaf parsley, chopped

- 2 tsp fresh dill, chopped
- Lemon wedges, to serve
- 1/3 cup olive oil
- 1/4 cup lemon juice

Directions:

1. Pre-heat griddle to medium heat.
2. Mix lemon juice with spinach in a bowl and set it aside.
3. Put olive oil on the fish and cook it for 3–4 minutes per side, or until it's done all the way through.
4. Take it off the heat, wrap it in foil, and let it sit for 5 minutes.
5. Add the rest of the oil and cook the spinach for two minutes, or until it is just wilted. Remove from the heat.
6. Toss with olives and herbs, then transfer to serving plates with fish, and serve with lemon wedges.

Nutrition:

Cal: 773 Fat: 36.6 g Carbs: 2.9 g Pro: 109.3 g

69. Pop-Open Clams with Horseradish-Tabasco Sauce

Prep: Ten Min

Cook: Three Min

Serves: 4

Ingredients:

- 1 tbsp fresh lemon juice
- 1 tbsp hot sauce, like Tabasco
- 1/4 tsp lemon zest, finely grated
- 1/4 tsp smoked paprika
- 2 dozen littleneck clams, scrubbed
- 2 tbsp horseradish, drained
- 4 tbsp unsalted butter, softened
- Sea salt

Directions:

1. Pre-heat the griddle to high.
2. Mix horseradish, hot sauce, lemon zest, lemon juice, paprika, and a pinch of salt into the butter.
3. Place the clams on the grill over high heat and cook until they open, which should take about 60 seconds.
4. Use tongs to carefully flip the clams over so that the meaty side is facing down.
5. Add another 60 seconds to the grilling time until the clam juices start to simmer.

6. Move the clams to a bowl for serving.
7. Add about 1/2 teaspoon of the sauce to each and serve.

Nutrition:

Cal: 191 Fat: 12.7 g Carbs: 4 g Pro: 14.8 g

70. Lemon Garlic Scallops

Prep: Ten Min

Cook: Five min

Serves: 3

Ingredients:

- 1 lb frozen bay scallops, thawed, rinsed and pat dry
- 1 tsp garlic, minced
- 1 tsp lemon juice
- 1 tsp parsley, chopped
- 2 tbsp olive oil
- Pepper and Salt

Directions:

1. Pre-heat the griddle to high heat.
2. Add oil to the griddle top.
3. Add garlic and sauté for 30 seconds.
4. Add scallops, lemon juice, pepper and salt, and sauté until scallops turn opaque.
5. Garnish with parsley and serve.

Nutrition:

Cal: 123 Fat: 14 g Carbs: 0.6 g Pro: 0.1 g

71. Tasty Shrimp Skewers

Prep: Five min

Cook: Ten Min

Serves: 3

Ingredients:

- 1 ½ lbs shrimp, peeled and deveined
- One tbsp dried oregano
- Two tsp garlic paste

- Two lemon juice
- 1/4 cup olive oil
- 1 tsp paprika
- Pepper and Salt

Directions:

1. Add all ingredients into the mixing bowl, mix well, and place in the refrigerator for 1 hour.
2. Remove marinated shrimp from the refrigerator and thread onto the skewers.
3. Pre-heat the griddle to high heat.
4. Place skewers onto the griddle top and cook for 5-7 mins.
5. Serve and relish.

Nutrition:

Cal: 212 Fat: 10.5 g Carbs: 2.7 g Pro: 26 g

72.   Salmon Lime Burgers

Prep: Fifteen Min

Cook: Ten Min

Serves: 2

Ingredients:

- 1 tbsp cilantro, fresh minced
- 1/2 lb. Salmon fillets, skinless, cubed
- Dijon mustard 1/2 tbsp
- grated lime zest 1/2 tbsp
- honey 1/2 tbsp
- soy sauce 1/2 tbsp

- 1/4 tsp sea salt, fine ground
- 1/8 tsp fresh ground pepper
- 1-1/2 garlic cloves, minced
- 1-1/2 tbsp shallots, finely chopped
- 2 hamburger buns, sliced in half

Directions:

1. Mix all of your ingredients in a mixing bowl, except the hamburger buns.
2. Make 2 burger patties that are 1/2-inch thick with this mixture.

3. Pre-heat your griddle grill in a medium-temperature setting.
4. Once your grill is Pre-heated, place the 2 patties on the grill.
5. Grill your patties for 5 mins per side. Serve on warm buns and relish!

Nutrition:

Cal: 220 Fat: 15 g Pro: 16 g Carbs: 6 g

73. Greek Salmon Fillets

Prep: Five min

Cook: Six min

Serves: 2

Ingredients:

- One tbsp butter, melted
- One tbsp fresh basil, minced
- One tbsp fresh lemon juice
- 1/8 tsp salt
- 2 salmon fillets

Directions:

1. Pre-heat the griddle to high heat.
2. Mix the lemon juice, basil, butter, and salt in a small bowl.
3. Put salmon fillets on a hot griddle top and brush them with the lemon mixture.
4. Two to three minutes is enough time to cook salmon. Flip the salmon and cook for another 2 to 3 mins.
5. Serve and relish.

Nutrition:

Cal: 290 Fat: 16.8 g Carbs: 0.3 g Pro: 34.7 g

74. Parmesan Shrimp

Prep: Five min

Cook: Six min

Serves: 6

Ingredients:

- 1 lb shrimp, peeled and deveined
- One garlic clove
- One tbsp fresh lemon juice
- One tbsp olive oil
- One tbsp pine nuts, toasted
- 1/2 cup basil
- 2 tbsp parmesan cheese, grated
- Pepper and Salt

Directions:

1. Add basil, lemon juice, cheese, pine nuts, garlic, pepper, and salt in a blender and blend until smooth.
2. Add shrimp and basil paste in a bowl and mix well.
3. Place shrimp bowl in the fridge for 20 mins.
4. Pre-heat the griddle to high heat.
5. Spray griddle top with cooking spray.
6. Thread marinated shrimp onto skewers and place skewers on the hot griddle top.
7. Cook shrimp for 3 mins on each side or until cooked.
8. Serve and relish.

Nutrition:

Cal: 225 Fat: 11.2 g Carbs: 2.2 g Pro: 27.2 g

75. Salmon Fillets with Basil Butter and Broccolini

Prep: Five min

Cook: Twenty Min

Serves: 2

Ingredients:

- 2 (6 ounces) salmon fillets, skin removed
- 2 tsp olive oil
- 2 tbsp butter, unsalted
- 2 basil leaves, minced
- 1 garlic clove, minced
- 6 ounces broccolini
- Sea salt, to taste

Directions:

1. Blend butter, basil, and garlic together until well-incorporated. Form into a ball and place in refrigerator until ready to serve.

2. Pre-heat griddle to medium-high heat.
3. Salt the salmon fillets on both sides and set them aside.
4. Put broccolini, a pinch of salt, and olive oil in a bowl, toss to coat, and set aside.
5. Brush the griddle with olive oil and cook the salmon for 12 minutes with the skin side down. Turn the salmon over and cook for 4 more minutes. Take it off the griddle and let it rest while you cook the broccolini.
6. Add the broccolini to the griddle, turning occasionally, until slightly charred, about 6 mins.
7. Top each salmon fillet with a slice of basil butter and serve with a side of broccolini.

Nutrition:

Cal: 398 Fat: 26.7 g Carbs: 6.2 g Pro: 35.6 g

76.   Lobster Tails With Lime Basil Butter

Prep: Five min

Cook: Nine Min

Serves: 4

Ingredients:

- 4 lobster tails (cut in half lengthwise)
- 3 tbsp olive oil

For the lime basil butter:

- 1 stick unsalted butter, softened
- 1 lime, zested and juiced
- 2 cloves garlic, minced

- Lime wedges (to serve)
- Sea salt, to taste

- 1/2 bunch basil, roughly chopped
- 1/4 tsp red pepper flakes

Directions:

1. Put the ingredients for the butter in a bowl and mix them together. Set the bowl aside until you're ready to use it.
2. Pre-heat griddle to medium-high heat.
3. Drizzle the lobster tail halves with olive oil and season with salt and pepper.
4. Place the lobster tails, flesh-side down, on the griddle.
5. Allow to cook until opaque, about 3 mins, flip and cook another 3 mins.
6. Add a dollop of the lime basil butter during the last minute of cooking.
7. Serve right away.

Nutrition:

Cal: 430 Fat: 34.7 g Carbs: 2.4 g Pro: 28 g

77.   Spicy Grilled Squid

Prep: Fifteen Min

Cook: Five min

Serves: 6

Ingredients:

- 1-1/2 lbs. Squid, prepared
-
For the marinade:

- 2 cloves garlic cloves, minced
- 3 tbsp gochujang
- 3 tbsp corn syrup
- 1 tsp yellow mustard
- 1 tsp soy sauce

- Olive oil

- 2 tsp sesame oil
- 1 tsp sesame seeds
- 2 green onions, chopped
- 1/2 tsp ginger, minced

Directions:

1. Pre-heat griddle to medium-high heat and brush with olive oil.
2. Add the squid and tentacles to the griddle and cook for 1 minute, or until the bottom is firm and opaque.
3. Turn them over and cook for another minute. If the body curls, use tongs to straighten it out.
4. Brush the squid with sauce and cook for two more minutes.
5. Turn the squid over and baste the other side. Cook for another minute, until the sauce is gone and the squid is shiny and red.

Nutrition:

Cal: 292 Fat: 8.6 g Carbs: 25.1 g Pro: 27.8 g

78.   Shrimp Veggie Stir Fry

Prep: Fifteen Min

Cook: Five min

Serves: 4

Ingredients:

- 1 cup mushrooms, sliced
- 1 cup tomatoes, diced
- 1 small onion, chopped
- 1 tbsp garlic, minced
- 1/2 lb shrimp, peeled and deveined
- 1/3 cup olives
- 2 tbsp olive oil
- Pepper and Salt

Directions:

1. Pre-heat the griddle to high heat. Add oil.
2. Add the onion, mushrooms, and garlic, and cook until the onion becomes soft.
3. Stir in the shrimp and tomatoes until the shrimp is done.
4. Put in the olives and mix well.
5. Take the pan off the heat and leave it alone for 5 minutes. Add pepper and salt to taste.
6. Serve and relish.

Nutrition:

Cal: 325 Fat: 18.7 g Carbs: 12.5 g Pro: 28.6 g

79. Coconut Pineapple Shrimp Skewers

Prep: Twenty Min

Cook: Twelve min

Serves: 6

Ingredients:

- 1 tbsp cilantro, chopped
- 4 tsp Tabasco Original Red Sauce
- 2 tsp soy sauce
- Olive oil, for grilling
- 1-1/2 pounds uncooked jumbo shrimp, peeled and deveined
- 1/2 cup light coconut milk
- 1/4 cup freshly squeezed orange juice
- 1/4 cup freshly squeezed lime juice (from about 2 large limes)
- 3/4-pound pineapple, cut into 1-inch chunks

Directions:

1. Combine the orange juice, lime juice, Tabasco sauce, cilantro, and coconut milk. Toss the shrimp in the mixture to coat.
2. To marinate for an hour, cover and put in the fridge.
3. Thread shrimp and pineapple onto metal skewers, alternating each.
4. Pre-heat griddle to medium heat.
5. Cook 5-6 mins, flipping once, until shrimp turn opaque pink.
6. Serve right away.

Nutrition:

Cal: 150 Fat: 10.8 g Carbs: 14.9 g Pro: 1.5 g

80.   Crab-stuffed Trout

Prep: Twenty Min

Cook: Fifteen Min

Serves: 2

Ingredients:

- 12 ounces crabmeat, picked over for shells and cartilage
- 1 cup chopped seeded fresh tomato, drained if necessary
- Grated zest of 1 lemon
- 1 tbsp good-quality olive oil, plus more for brushing the fish
- 2 scallions, trimmed and chopped
- Salt and pepper
- 4 8- to 10-ounce rainbow trout, cleaned and butterflied
- Lemon wedges for serving

Directions:

1. Preparing the Ingredients
2. In a medium bowl, combine the crab, tomato, and lemon zest. In a small pan over medium heat, add the oil and scallions; cook, turning regularly, for two to three minutes, or until softened. Add to the crab, season with salt and pepper, mix gently, taste, and make any necessary seasoning adjustments.
3. Pat the trout dry with paper towels. Brush them with oil and sprinkle with salt and pepper on both sides. Divide the crab mixture between the trout, filling their cavities. Pull the two sides closed, pushing the filling in, if needed, to keep it from spilling out.

4. Bring the griddle grill to high heat, Oil the griddle, and allow it to heat. Put the trout with the open side of the fish facing you, and cook until the skin browns and the fish release easily, 8 to 10 Mins. Carefully turn the fish, using a second spatula to lower them back down to the grates. Close the lid and cook until the stuffing is heated through and a skewer or thin knife inserted at the thickest point of a fish easily pierces it all the way through, 4 to 5 Mins. Transfer the trout to a platter and serve with lemon wedges.

Nutrition:

Cal 41 Fat 0.2 g Carbs 8 g Pro 1 g

81.Lemon Garlic Shrimp

Prep: Fifteen Min

Cook: Eight Min

Serves: 5

Ingredients:

- 1 1/2 lbs shrimp, peeled and deveined
- 1 tbsp garlic, minced
- 1/4 cup butter
- 1/4 cup fresh lemon juice
- 1/4 cup fresh parsley, chopped
- Pepper and Salt

Directions:

1. Pre-heat the griddle to high heat.
2. Melt butter on the griddle top.
3. Add garlic and sauté for sixty seconds.
4. Add shrimp and season with pepper and salt and cook for 4-5 mins or until it turns pink.
5. Add lemon juice and parsley and stir well and cook for 2 mins.
6. Serve and relish.

Nutrition:

Cal: 312 Fat: 14.6 g Carbs: 3.9 g Pro: 39.2 g

Chapter 11.   Parties

82.   Griddle Layered Cake

Prep: Ten min

Cook: Twenty min

Serves: 6

Ingredients:

- ¼ cup melted butter
- 1 cup of blueberries
- 1 cup of raspberries
- 1 cup sliced strawberries
- 2 x pound cake
- 3 cups of whipped cream

Directions:

1. Pre-heat the griddle to high with a closed lid.
2. Slice cake loaf (3/4 inch), about 10 per loaf.
3. Brush both sides with butter.
4. Griddle for 7 mins on each side.
5. Set aside.
6. Once cooled completely, start layering your cake.
7. Place cake berries, then cream.
8. Sprinkle with berries and Serve.

Nutrition:

Cal: 160, Pro: 2.3g, Carbs: 22g, Fat: 6g

83.   Seasonal Fruit on the Griddle

Prep: Five min

Cook: Ten min

Serves: 4

Ingredients:

- 2 plums, peaches apricots, etc. (choose seasonally)
- 3 tbsp Sugar, turbinate
- ¼ cup of Honey
- Gelato, as desired

Directions:

1. Pre-heat the griddle to 450°F with a closed lid.
2. Slice each fruit in halves and remove the pits.
3. Brush with honey.
4. Sprinkle with some sugar.
5. Griddle on the grate until you see that there are griddle marks.
6. Set aside.
7. Serv each with a scoop of gelato.
8. Enjoy.

Nutrition:

Cal: 120, Pro: 1g, Carbs: 15g, Fat: 3g

84.   Caramel Bananas

Prep: Fifteen min

Cook: Fifteen min

Serves: 4

Ingredients:

- 1/3 cup chopped pecans
- ½ cup sweetened condensed milk
- 4 slightly green bananas
- ½ cup brown sugar
- 2 tbsp corn syrup
- ½ cup butter

Directions:

1. Pre-heat your griddle with the lid closed until it reaches 350°F.
2. Place milk, corn syrup, butter, and brown sugar into a heavy saucepan
3. Bring to boil. For 5 mins simmer the mixture on low heat.
4. Stir frequently.
5. Place bananas with peels on the griddle and let them griddle for five mins.
6. Flip and cook for five mins more.
7. Peels will be dark and might split.
8. Place on a serving platter.

9. Cut ends off the bananas and split peel down the middle.
10. Take the peel off the bananas and spoon caramel on top.
11. Sprinkle with pecans.

Nutrition:

Cal: 152, Carbs: 36g, Fat: 1g, Pro: 1g

85. Bacon and Egg Wraps with Salsa

Prep: Fifteen min

Cook: Ten min

Serves: 3

Ingredients:

- 3corn tortillas
- 3slices bacon, cut into strips
- 2scrambled eggs
- 3tbsp salsa
- 1 cup grated Pepper Jack cheese
- 2tbsp cream cheese, divided
- Cooking spray

Directions:

1. Spritz the perforated pan with cooking spray.
2. Unfold the tortillas on a clean work surface, divide the bacon and eggs in the middle of the tortillas, then spread with salsa and scatter with cheeses.
3. Fold the tortillas over.
4. Arrange tortillas in the pan.
5. Select Air Fry. Set temperature to 390°F (199°C) and set Time to 10 mins.
6. Press Start to begin Pre-heating.
7. Once the oven has Pre-heated, place the pan into the oven.
8. Flip tortillas halfway through the Cook.
9. When cooking is complete, the cheeses will be melted and the tortillas will be lightly browned.
10. Serve right away.

Nutrition:

Cal 290, Fat 10.5g, Carbs 23.2g, Pro 27.3g

86. Tortilla Pizza

Prep: Ten min

Cook: Five min

Serves: 1

Ingredients:

- 1 tortilla
- For topping:
- 1/4 tsp red chili flakes
- 1/4 tsp dried oregano
- 1/2 tsp garlic, minced
- 2 tsp onion, chopped
- 1/4 cup tomatoes, chopped
- 3 tbsp mozzarella cheese, shredded
- Salt and pepper to taste

Directions:

1. Add tomatoes, onion, garlic, oregano, chili flakes, cheese, pepper, and salt to a tortilla.
2. Pre-heat the griddle to high heat.
3. Spray griddle top with cooking spray.
4. Place tortilla on hot griddle top, cover and cook until cheese melts.

Nutrition:

Cal 336, Fat 15.8 g, Carbs 18 g, Pro 26.1 g

87.   Brussel Sprouts, Mango, Avocado Salsa Tacos

Prep: Twenty-Five min

Cook: Fifteen min

Serves: 4

Ingredients:

- ½ of mango, diced
- ½l of an avocado, diced
- 1 tbsp. jalapeno, chopped
- 1 tbsp. taco seasoning
- 1/2 cup black beans, cooked
- 1/4 cup cilantro, chopped
- 2 tbsp. Olive oil
- 2 tbsp. onions, chopped
- 4 taco shells
- 8 ounces brussels sprouts, diced
- Lime juice of 1 lime
- Salt & Pepper to taste

Directions:

1. Mix the sprouts with taco seasoning, olive oil, salt, and pepper on the pan.
2. Roast for 15 mins. Turn every 5 mins.
3. To make salsa, add mango, avocado, black beans, lime juice, cilantro, onion, jalapeno, salt, and pepper.
4. Cook taco shells and fill them with sprouts and salsa.

Nutrition:

Cal 407kcal, Carbs: 63.20g, Pro: 11.4g, Fat: 13.9g.

88.   Ultimate Burrito

Prep: Five min

Cook: Twenty min

Serves: 2

Ingredients:

- 1 large russet potato, peeled and cut into small cubes
- 1 red bell pepper
- 1 ripe avocado, sliced
- 1/2 yellow onion

- 2 large flour tortillas
- 2 tbsp hot sauce
- 2 tbsp. vegetable oil
- 4 eggs
- 4 strips bacon

Directions:

1. Pre-heat the griddle to medium-high heat on one side and medium heat on the other side.
2. Brush with vegetable oil
3. Add bacon to the medium heat side and peppers and onions to the medium-high side.
4. When bacon finishes cooking, place on paper towels and chop into small pieces.
5. Add potatoes to the bacon fat on the griddle.
6. Cook potatoes until softened.
7. Add eggs to the vegetable side and cook until firm.
8. Place ingredients onto the tortillas and top with slices of avocado and a tbsp of hot sauce.
9. Fold the tortillas and enjoy.

Nutrition:

Cal: 793, Fat: 41.3.g, Carbs: 73.4g Pro: 35.8g

89.   Zucchini Hummus Wrap

Prep: Ten min

Cook: Eight min

Serves: 2

Ingredients:

- ½ cup iceberg lettuce
- 1 zucchini, sliced
- 2 cherry tomatoes, sliced
- 2 spelt flour tortillas
- 4 tbsp homemade hummus
- Extra:
- ¼ tsp salt
- 1 tbsp grapeseed oil
- 1/8 tsp cayenne pepper

Directions:

1. Take a grill pan, grease it with oil and let it Pre-heat over a medium-high heat setting.
2. Meanwhile, place zucchini slices, and
3. Add a pinch of salt and cayenne pepper, splash some oil over it, and toss to coat.
4. Slices of zucchini should be placed on the grill pan and cooked for 2 to 3 minutes on each side, or until grill marks appear.
5. Assemble tortillas and heat the tortilla on the grill pan until warm, develop grill marks, and spread 2 tbsp of hummus over each tortilla.
6. Distribute grilled zucchini slices over the tortillas, top with lettuce and tomato slices, and then wrap tightly.

Nutrition:

Cal 264.5; Fats 5.1 g; Pro 8.5 g; Carbs 34.5 g;

90. Cheesy Jalapeño Griddle Dip

Prep: Ten min

Cook: Fifteen min

Serves: 8

Ingredients:

- 8 ounces cream cheese
- 16 ounces shredded cheese
- 1/3 cup mayonnaise
- 4 ounces diced green chilies
- 3 fresh jalapeños
- 2 tsp Killer Hogs AP Rub
- 2 tsp Mexican Style Seasoning
- For the topping:
- ¼ cup Mexican Blend Shredded Cheese
- Sliced jalapeños

- Mexican Style Seasoning
- 3 tbsp Killer Hogs AP Rub
- 2 tbsp Chili Powder
- 2 tbsp Paprika
- 2 tsp Cumin
- ½ tsp Granulated Onion
- ¼ tsp Cayenne Pepper
- ¼ tsp Chipotle Chili Pepper ground
- ¼ tsp Oregano

Directions:

1. Pre-heat griddle or flame broil for roundabout cooking at 350°F.
2. Join fixings in a big bowl and spot in a cast to press griddle
3. Top with Mexican Blend destroyed cheddar and cuts of jalapeno's
4. Spot iron griddle on flame broil mesh and cook until cheddar hot and bubbly and the top has seared
5. Marginally about 25mins.
6. Serve warm with enormous corn chips (scoops), tortilla chips, or your preferred vegetables for plunging.

Nutrition:

Cal: 150, Carbs: 22g, Fat: 6g, Pro: 3g

91. Veggie Salsa Wraps

Prep: Five min

Cook: Seven min

Serves: 4

Ingredients:

- 1 cup red onion, sliced
- 1 zucchini, chopped
- 1 poblano pepper, deseeded and finely chopped
- 1 head lettuce
- ½ cup salsa
- 8ounces (227 g) Mozzarella cheese

Directions:

1. Place red onion, zucchini, and poblano pepper von the Grill.
2. Cook at 390°F (199°C) for 7 mins, or until y are tender and fragrant.
3. Spoon the salsa on top of the lettuce leaves after dividing the veggie mixture among them.
4. Finish off with Mozzarella cheese.
5. Wrap the lettuce leaves around filling.
6. Serve right away.

Nutrition:

Cal 140, Fat 4g, Carbs 5g, Pro 7g

92.   Griddle Fruit with Cream

Prep: Fifteen min

Cook: Ten min

Serves: 6

Ingredients:

- 2 halved Apricot
- 1 halved Nectarine
- 2 halved peaches
- ¼ cup of Blueberries
- ½ cup of Raspberries
- 2 tbsp of Honey

- 1 orange, the peel
- 2 cups of Cream

- ½ cup of Balsamic Vinegar

Directions:

1. Pre-heat the griddle to 400°F with a closed lid.
2. Griddle the peaches, nectarines, and apricots for 4 mins on each side.
3. Turn the heat to medium and place a pan on the stove.
4. Add 2 tbsp of honey, vinegar, and orange peel.
5. Simmer until medium thick.
6. In the meantime, add honey and cream in a bowl.
7. Whip until it reaches a soft form.
8. Place fruits on a serving plate. Sprinkle with berries.
9. Drizzle with balsamic reduction. Serve with cream and enjoy!

Nutrition:

Cal: 230, Pro: 3g, Carbs: 35g, Fat: 3g

93.   Blueberry Cobbler

Prep: Fifteen min

Cook: Thirty min

Serves: 6

Ingredients:

- ¼ tsp salt
- ¾ cup whole milk
- 1 cup all-purpose flour, plus 2 tbsp.
- 1 cup sugar, plus 2 tbsp.
- 1 tsp. grated lemon zest

- 1/8 tsp ground cinnamon
- 2 tsp. baking powder
- 4 cups fresh blueberries
- 6 tbsp unsalted butter
- Juice of 1 lemon

Directions:

2. Add blueberries, lemon zest, two tablespoons of sugar, two tablespoons of flour, and lemon juice to a medium bowl.
3. Add the remaining 1 cup of flour, 1 cup of sugar, baking powder, and salt to another medium-sized bowl.
4. Blend butter into flour mixture until a uniform crumb texture is achieved. Milk should be added and stirred until dough forms.

5. choose BAKE, Set the timer for 30 minutes and the temperature to 350°F. To start the Pre-heating process, choose START/STOP.
6. Meanwhile, pour the blueberry mixture into the Multi-Purpose Pan. Spread it evenly across the pan.
7. Gently pour the batter over the blueberry mixture, and, then sprinkle cinnamon over the top.
8. If the unit beeps to signify it has Pre-heated, place pan directly in the pot.
9. Close hood and cook for 30 mins, until lightly golden.
10. When cooking is complete, serve warm.

Nutrition:

Cal: 408, fat: 8g, Carbs: 72g, Pro: 5g

94.   Juicy Loosey Cheeseburger

Prep: Ten min

Cook: Ten min

Serves: 6

Ingredients:

- 1 Cup dry bread crumbs
- 1 egg beaten
- 1 tbsp Griddle Griddles All Purpose Rub
- 2 lbs. ground beef
- 2 tbsp Worcestershire sauce
- 3 tbsp evaporated milk
- 4 buns
- 4 slices of cheddar cheese

Directions:

1. Start by mixing together dating the hamburger, egg, dissipated milk, and Worcestershire and focus on a bowl. Use your hands to blend well.
2. Divide the blend into 4 equivalent parts. At that point, take every one of the 4 sections and partition them into equal parts.
3. Take every one of these little parts and smooth them.
4. The objective is to have 8 equivalent level patties that you will then join into 4 burgers.
5. When you have your patties smoothed, place your cheddar in the center and afterward, place the other patty over this and firmly squeeze the sides to seal.
6. You may even need to push the meat back towards the inside piece to shape a marginally thicker patty.
7. The patties ought to be marginally bigger than a standard burger bun as they will recoil a bit of during cooking.

8. Pre-heat your Kong to 300°F.
9. Keep in mind during flame broiling that you have two meager patties, one on each side, so the cooking time ought not to have a place.
10. You will Cook se for 5 to 8mins per side—closer to 5mins on the off chance that you favor an uncommon burger or more towards 8mins if you like a well to done burger.
11. At the point when you Flip burgers, take a toothpick and penetrate the focal point of the burger to allow the steam to evaporate.

12. This will prevent you from having a hit to out or having a visitor who gets a jaw consume from liquid cheddar as they Take its first nibble.
13. Toss these on a pleasant roll and top with fixings that supplement whatever your burgers are loaded down with.

Nutrition:

Cal: 300, Carbs: 33g, Fat: 12g, Pro: 15g

95.　　Apple Pie on the Griddle

Prep: Fifteen min

Cook: Thirty min

Serves: 6

Ingredients:

- ¼ cup of Sugar
- 4 Apples, sliced
- 1 tbsp of Cornstarch
- 1 tsp Cinnamon, ground

- 1 Pie Crust, refrigerated, soften in according to the directions on the box
- ½ cup of Peach preserves

Directions:

10. Pre-heat the griddle to 375°F with a closed lid.
11. In a bowl, add cinnamon, cornstarch, sugar, and apples and set it aside.
12. Place pie crust in a pie pan.
13. Set preserve s and then place apples.
14. Fold the crust slightly.
15. Place a pan on the griddle (upside-down) so that you don't brill/bake the pie directly on the heat.
16. Cook 30 - 40 mins.
17. Once done, set aside to rest. Serve and enjoy

Nutrition:

Cal: 160, Pro: 0.5g, Carbs: 35g, Fat: 1g

96.   Chicken Tacos with Avocado Crema

Prep: One Hour Five min

Cook: Ten min

Serves: 4-5

Ingredients:

- 1 ½lbs. Boneless, skinless chicken breasts, sliced thin
- 1 lime, juiced
- 1 serrano pepper, minced
- 1 tsp ground cumin
- 1/3 cup olive oil
- 2 tsp garlic, minced
- Black pepper, to taste
- For the chicken marinade:
- Sea salt, to taste
- For the avocado crema:
- 1 cup sour cream
- 2 tsp lime juice
- 1 tsp lime zest
- 1 serrano pepper, diced and seeded
- 1 clove garlic, minced
- 1 large hass avocado
- For the garnish:
- 1 lime sliced into wedges
- 1/2 cup queso fresco, crumbled
- 10 corn tortillas
- 2 tsp cilantro, chopped

Directions:

1. Mix chicken marinade together in a sealable plastic bag.
2. Add chicken and toss to coat well.
3. Marinate for 1 hour in the refrigerator.
4. Combine avocado crema ingredients in a food processor or blender and pulse until smooth.
5. Cover and refrigerate until you are ready to assemble tacos.
6. Pre-heat griddle to medium heat and grill chicken for 5 mins per side, rotating and turning as needed.
7. Remove from griddle and tent loosely with aluminum foil.
8. Allow chicken to cool for 5 mins.
9. Serve with warm tortillas, a dollop of avocado crema, queso fresco, cilantro and lime wedges.

Nutrition:

Cal: 703, Fat: 44.5 g, Carbs: 30.5g, Pro: 47.

97.   Cod Tacos with Salsa

Prep: Five min

Cook: Fifteen min

Serves: 4

Ingredients:

- 2 eggs
- 1¼ cups Mexican beer
- 11/2 cups coconut flour
- 11/2 cups almond flour
- 1/2 tbsp chili powder
- 1 tbsp cumin
- Salt, to taste
- 1 pound (454 g) cod fillet, slice into large pieces
- 4 toasted corn tortillas
- 4 large lettuce leaves, chopped
- ¼ cup salsa
- Cooking spray

Directions:

1. Spritz the air fry basket with cooking spray.
2. Break the eggs in a bowl, then pour in the beer.
3. Whisk to combine well.
4. Combine almond flour, coconut flour, cumin, chili powder, and salt in a separate bowl. Stir to mix well.
5. Dunk the cod pieces in the egg mixture, then shake the excess off and dredge into the flour mixture to coat well.
6. Arrange cod in the basket.
7. Place basket on the air fry position.
8. Select Air Fry, set the temperature to 375°F (190°C) and set Time to 15 mins.
9. Flip cod halfway through the cooking time.
10. When cooking is complete, the cod should be golden brown.
11. Unwrap toasted tortillas on a large plate, then divide the cod and lettuce leaves on top.
12. Baste with salsa and wrap to serve.

Nutrition:

Cal 133, Fat 19g, Carbs 17g, Pro 8g

98.   Cod Fish Tacos with Mango Salsa

Prep: Fifteen min

Cook: Seventeen min

Serves: 6 tacos

Ingredients:

- ¼ tsp chili powder
- ½ pound cod, cut into large pieces
- ½ tsp ground cumin
- ¾ cup all-purpose flour
- ¾ cup cornstarch
- 1 egg
- 5ounces Mexican beer
- 6corn tortillas
- Cooking spray

- Salsa:
- ¼ red bell pepper, diced
- ¼ red onion, minced
- ¼ tsp ground black pepper
- ¼ tsp salt
- ½ small jalapeño, diced
- 1 mango, peeled and diced
- Juice of half a lime
- Pinch chopped fresh cilantro

Directions:

1. Spritz the perforated pan with cooking spray.
2. Whisk the egg with a beer in a bowl.
3. Mix
4. Dredge the cod in the egg mixture first, then in the flour mixture to coat well.
5. Shake the excess off.
6. Arrange cod in the perforated pan and spritz with cooking spray.
7. Select Air Fry. Set the temperature to 380°F (193°C) and set Time to 17 mins.
8. Press Start to begin Pre-heating.
9. Once Pre-heated, place the pan into the oven.
10. Flip cod halfway through the cooking time.
11. When cooked, the cod should be golden brown and crunchy.
12. Meanwhile, add Ingredients for the salsa in a small bowl.
13. Stir to mix well.
14. Unfold the tortillas on a clean work surface, divide the fish between the tortillas, and Set salsa on top.
15. Fold to serve.

Nutrition:

Cal 126, Fat 12.1g, Carbs 2.8g, Pro 2.1g

Chapter 12.   Meats

99.   Grilled Lemon Veal Chops

Prep: Fifteen–Thirty min

Serves: 4

Cook: Ten min

Ingredients:

- 4 bone-in rib veal chops
- 6 tbsp. lemon juice, freshly squeezed
- 3 tbsp. minced garlic
- 2 tbsp. lemon zest, grated
- Salt and pepper to taste
- Olive oil, for brushing

Directions:

1. Place all ingredients in a bowl and marinate the veal in the fridge for at least 6 hours.
2. Heat the griddle pan over medium heat and brush with oil.
3. Cook the veal for 5 mins on each side.

Nutrition:

Cal: 312 Pro: 22 g Carbs: 3 g Fat: 8 g

100.   Smoked Pork Brisket

Prep: Fifteen–Thirty min

Serves: 5

Cook: Fifteen min

Ingredients:

- 3 lbs. pork brisket, sliced to 1-inch thick
- ¾ cup pork seasoning
- 2 tbsp. liquid smoke seasoning
- Olive oil, for brushing

Directions:

1. Season the pork with the seasonings.
2. Heat the griddle pan to medium heat and brush with oil.
3. Cook on all sides for 10 to 15 mins while stirring constantly.

Nutrition:

Cal: 247 Pro: 27 g Carbs: 0 g Fat: 8 g

101. Tuscan-Style Veal Chops

Prep: Fifteen–Thirty min

Serves: 4

Cook: Ten min

Ingredients:

- ¼ cup sage leaves, chopped
- 1 tbsp. rosemary leaves, chopped
- 2 garlic cloves, minced
- 2 tbsp. extra-virgin olive oil
- 4 12-oz. veal ribs
- Salt and pepper to taste

Directions:

1. Brush some olive oil on the griddle pan and heat it over medium heat.
2. In a bowl, combine the sage, rosemary, and garlic.
3. Season the veal to taste with salt and pepper after rubbing the herb mixture on it.
4. Cook for 5 minutes on each side on the griddle.

Nutrition:

Cal: 724 Pro: 67 g Carbs: 7 g Fat: 48 g

102. Grilled Antelope Backstrap Butterfly Steaks

Prep: Fifteen–Thirty min

Serves: 4

Cook: Ten min

Ingredients:

- 2 tbsp. olive oil
- 2 lb. antelope Backstrap
- Salt to taste

Directions:

1. Heat the griddle pan and brush with oil.
2. Season the antelope meat with salt to taste.
3. Sear for 5 mins on each side.

Nutrition:

Cal: 338 Pro: 51 g Carbs: 0 g Fat: 11 g

103. Grilled Venison with Mushrooms

Prep: Fifteen–Thirty min

Serves: 4

Cook: Ten min

Ingredients:

- 1 tbsp. olive oil
- 3 garlic cloves, minced
- 1 onion, chopped
- 4 venison tenderloin medallions, cut into 1-inch thick
- Salt and pepper to taste
- 4 oz. cremini mushrooms, sliced
- 1 tsp. Dijon mustard
- ½ green onion stalk, minced

Directions:

1. On the griddle pan, heat the olive oil over medium-low heat.
2. After adding the onion and garlic, sauté for two minutes.
3. Season the venison with salt and pepper to taste before adding it.
4. Stir for 3 mins then add the mushrooms.
5. Season with Dijon and cook for another 8 mins.
6. Garnish with green onions.

Nutrition:

Cal: 192 Pro: 12 g Carbs: 26 g Fat: 6 g

104.   Roast Beef Sandwich

Prep: Ten min

Cook: Five min

Serves: 1

Ingredients:

- 2 bread slices
- 2 cheese slices
- 4 deli roast beef, sliced
- 2 tsp butter
- 1 tbsp mayonnaise
- 1/4 cup caramelized onions, sliced

Directions:

1. Spread butter on one side of each bread slice.
2. Take 1 bread slice and spread with mayo top with beef, onion, and cheese.
3. Cover with remaining bread slice.
4. Pre-heat the griddle to high heat.
5. Spray griddle top with cooking spray.
6. Place sandwich on hot griddle top and cook for 5 mins or until golden brown from both sides.
7. Serve and enjoy.

Nutrition:

Cal 859 Fat 44.6 g Carbs 25.4 g Pro 83.4 g

105.   Garlic Butter Lamb Chops

Prep: Fifteen–Thirty min

Serves: 2

Cook: Ten min

Ingredients:

- 1 tsp. salt
- ½ tsp. black pepper
- 1 tsp. minced garlic
- 8 tbsp. butter, room temperature
- 1 pack French lamb ribs
- ¼ cup fresh herbs of your choice, chopped

Directions:

1. In a bowl, mix the salt, pepper, garlic, and butter until well combined.
2. Brush all over the lamb.
3. Set the griddle pan on medium-high heat then place the lamb on the griddle.
4. Allow it to sear and cook for 5 mins per side.
5. Serve with chopped herbs.

Nutrition:

Cal: 290 Pro: 7 g Carbs: 1 g Fat: 29 g

106.   Grilled Veal Chops

Prep: Fifteen–Thirty min

Serves: 4

Cook: Ten min

Ingredients:

- 1 tbsp. olive oil
- 2 lb. veal chops
- 4 garlic cloves, minced
- 1 lemon zested
- Salt and pepper to taste
- 1 ½ tbsp. rosemary leaves, chopped

Directions:

1. Heat the griddle pan and brush with oil.
2. Place all ingredients in a bowl and toss to season all sides of the chops.

3. Cook the chops on the griddle pan for 5 mins on each side.
4. Allow them to rest before slicing.

Nutrition:

Cal: 424 Pro: 44 g Carbs: 6 g Fat: 9 g

107. Grilled Stuff Pork Chops

Prep: Fifteen–Thirty min

Serves: 4

Cook: Eighteen min

Ingredients:

- 4 thick-cut pork chops
- 10 oz. chopped spinach, blanched
- 4 oz. grated Parmesan cheese
- 1 shallot, chopped
- 1 tbsp. dried thyme
- 1 tbsp. paprika
- Salt and pepper to taste
- Olive oil, for brushing

Directions:

1. Cut a slit on the meaty side of the pork chops to create a pocket. Set aside.
2. In a bowl, mix the spinach, Parmesan cheese, shallot, thyme, and paprika. Mix until well combined.
3. Place the spinach mixture inside the meat. Use a toothpick to adhere the ends.
4. Put salt and pepper on the meat to season it.
5. Brush oil on the griddle and heat to medium.
6. Cook the pork chops for nine minutes on each side.

Nutrition:

Cal: 467 Pro: 47 g Carbs: 11 g Fat: 11 g

108. Griddled Lamb Steak with Caramelized Celeriac

Prep: Fifteen–Thirty min

Serves: 6

Cook: Ten min

Ingredients:

- 2 tbsp. olive oil
- 1 celeriac, peeled and shaved
- 3 lb. lamb steak
-
- Salt and pepper to taste
- 1 cup chopped mint

Directions:

1. Caramelize the celeriac by sautéing it in olive oil on a griddle. Place aside.
2. Add salt and pepper to the lamb steak before serving.
3. For three minutes on each side, sear the lamb steak on the griddle.
4. Serve with chopped mint and celeriac.

Nutrition:

Cal: 383 Pro: 55 g Carbs: 1 g Fat: 18 g

109.   Korean Ground Beef Rice Bowl

Prep: Fifteen–Thirty min

Cook: Fifteen min

Serves: 4

Ingredients:

- ¼ cup ground beef
- ¼ cup light brown soy sauce
- ½ tsp. crushed red pepper flakes
- 2 cups cooked brown rice
- 2 tbsp. olive oil
- 2 tsp. sesame oil
- Chopped scallion, for garnish
- Salt and pepper to taste

Directions:

1. Heat the griddle to 300°F and pour in the oil.
2. Cook the beef and stir until golden brown. Season with salt, pepper, and soy sauce.
3. Add in the red pepper flakes and stir in the rice.
4. Keep stirring until well combined.

5. Add in the sesame oil and scallions and stir for another 3 mins.
6. Serve.

Nutrition:

Cal: 256 Pro: 18 g Carbs: 4 g Fat: 18 g

110. Honey-Mustard Marinated Pork Chops

Prep: Fifteen–Thirty min

Cook: Ten min

Serves: 2

Ingredients:

- ½ tsp. ground pepper
- 1 tsp. honey
- 1 tsp. soy sauce
- 1 tsp. wet mustard
- 2 center-cut pork chops
- 2 dashes Worcestershire sauce
- Olive oil, for brushing

Directions:

1. Marinate the pork chops with mustard, honey, soy sauce, ground pepper, and Worcestershire sauce.
2. Marinate for 6 hours in the fridge.
3. Heat the griddle pan to medium and brush with oil.
4. Cook the pork chops for 5 mins on each side.
5. Allow them to rest before slicing.

Nutrition:

Cal: 251 Pro: 40 g Carbs: 5 g Fat: 7 g

111. Rosemary Lamb Chops

Prep: Fifteen–Thirty min

Cook: Ten min

Serves: 8

Ingredients:

- 8 lamb chops
- 1 tsp. salt
-
- 1 tbsp. chopped rosemary leaves
- 1 tbsp. garlic powder

Directions:

1. Season the lamb chops with salt, rosemary leaves, and garlic powder.
2. Heat the grill to medium-high heat and sear the lamb chops for 5 mins on each side.
3. Allow the lamb chops to rest before slicing.

Nutrition:

Cal: 326 Pro: 46 g Carbs: 1 g Fat: 16 g

112.   Tandoori Pork

Prep: Fifteen–Thirty min

Cook: Ten min

Serves: 4

Ingredients:

- 1 tbsp. ground coriander
- 1 tbsp. ground cumin
- 1 tbsp. paprika
- 1 tsp. ground fenugreek seeds
- 12 garlic cloves, minced
- 2 ½ tsp. garam masala
- 2 tsp. Indian chili paste
- 4 14-oz. pork loin
- 4-inch ginger, grated
- 5 tbsp. lemon juice
- Olive oil, for brushing

For Serving:

- Naan bread
- Yogurt
- Sliced cucumbers

Directions:

1. Combine all the ingredients in a dish and stir until the seasoning is evenly distributed over the pork loin. Marinate for at least 12 hours in the refrigerator.
2. Oil the griddle pan and heat it over medium heat.
3. Cook the pork chops for 5 mins on each side.
4. Serve the meat with naan bread, yogurt, and sliced cucumbers.

Nutrition:

Cal: 845 Pro: 112 g Carbs: 7 g Fat: 38 g

113.   Easy Griddled Pork Chops

Prep: Fifteen–Thirty min

Cook: Ten min

Serves: 2

Ingredients:

- 2 center-cut boneless pork chops
- 2 tsp. extra-virgin olive oil
- Salt and pepper to taste

Directions:

1. Brush the pork chops with oil and season with salt and pepper to taste.
2. Heat the griddle pan and brush the pan with oil.
3. Cook for 5 mins on each side.
4. Remove the pork chops and allow them to rest for 5 mins.

Nutrition:

Cal: 253 Pro: 40 g Carbs: 2 g Fat: 9 g

114.   Mustard & Rosemary Pork Chops

Prep: Fifteen–Thirty min

Cook: Eighteen min

Serves: 4

Ingredients:

- 2 tbsp. mild mustard
- 3 tbsp. olive oil
- 1 garlic clove, sliced
- 2 sprigs rosemary, chopped
- 1 tbsp. sherry or balsamic vinegar
- 4 pork shoulder
- Olive oil, for brushing

Directions:

1. In a bowl, mix the mustard, olive oil, garlic, rosemary, and balsamic vinegar.
2. Brush the pork with the seasoning mixture.
3. Heat the griddle to medium and brush with oil.
4. Cook the pork for 7 to 9 mins on each side.

Nutrition:

Cal: 506 Pro: 42 g Carbs: 2 g Fat: 37 g

115. Pulled Pork Griddle Cakes

Prep: Fifteen–Thirty min

Cook: Twelve min

Serves: 8

Ingredients:

- ½ cup all-purpose flour
- 1 ½ cup self-rising white cornmeal mix
- 1 2/3 cup buttermilk
- 1 tbsp. sugar
- 2 cups leftover pulled pork
- 2 large eggs, beaten
- 3 tbsp. butter, melted

Directions:

1. Brushing the pan with oil before heating it up over medium heat.
2. All ingredients should be mixed thoroughly in a bowl.
3. Pour ½ cup of the batter on the griddle pot and cook for 3 mins on each side.
4. Repeat until all batter is cooked.

Nutrition:

Cal: 250 Pro: 14 g Carbs: 29 g Fat: 8 g

116.   London Broil

Prep: Fifteen–Thirty min

Cook: Eighteen

Serves: 8

Ingredients:

- 2 lb. London broil
- 1 cup dry red wine
- Salt and pepper to taste

Directions:

1. Score the meat with a fork.
2. Pour the red wine in and place in a Ziploc bag. Refrigerate for 24 hours while marinating.
3. For five minutes, heat the griddle pan.
4. Salt and pepper the meat after removing it from the marinade.
5. On the griddle, fry the meat for 6 minutes on each side.
6. Verify that the interior temperature is 135 degrees Fahrenheit.
7. Allow the meat to rest before slicing.

Nutrition:

Cal: 239 Pro: 35 g Carbs: 0.64 g Fat: 10 g

117.   Masala Lamb Chops

Prep: Fifteen–Thirty min

Cook: Ten min

Serves: 4

Ingredients:

- 4 lamb chops
- Salt and pepper to taste
- 2 tbsp. curry powder
- 1 tsp. red pepper flakes
- 1 small red onion, chopped
-

- 1 large tomato, chopped
- 1 cup Greek yogurt
- 2 tbsp Chopped coriander
- Lemon, sliced, for serving
- Olive oil, for brushing

Directions:

1. Heat the griddle pan to high heat. Brush with oil.
2. Season the lamb chops with salt, pepper, curry powder, and red pepper flakes.
3. Sear the lamb chops for 3 to 5 mins on each side.
4. Meanwhile, mix the red onion, tomatoes, yogurt, and coriander in a bowl.
5. Serve the lamb chops with the yogurt mixture and slices of lemon.

Nutrition:

Cal: 231 Pro: 26 g Carbs: 10 g Fat: 10 g

118. Teriyaki Grilled Venison Medallions

Prep: Fifteen–Thirty min

Cook: Eight min

Serves: 4

Ingredients:

- ¼ tsp. powdered ginger
- ½ tsp. powdered garlic
- ½ tsp. rice vinegar
- 1 tbsp. extra-virgin olive oil

- 1 tbsp. honey
- 1 tbsp. toasted sesame oil
- 4 tbsp. soy sauce
- 4 venison tenderloin medallions, sliced to 1-inch thick

Directions:

1. All the ingredients—aside from the olive oil—should be thoroughly mixed in a dish.
2. For at least 6 hours, let them marinade in the refrigerator.
3. Brush some olive oil on the griddle pan and heat it up to medium.
4. Sear the venison for 8 mins.

5. Keep stirring until done.

Nutrition:

Cal: 165 Pro: 9 g Carbs: 8 g Fat: 10.2 g

Conclusion

Thank you for making it to the end. A gas grill is an outdoor cooking tool that you can use to cook various dishes from steaks to vegetables. You can find a gas grill at most hardware or home supply stores, and it's not too expensive. These grills come in different shapes and sizes, so you'll have to decide what's best for your needs based on the type of stove top you have.

There are a lot of accessories that you'll need with your new grill, but the best one is a cover. Covering your grill will help protect it from environmental hazards such as leaves and tree sap that could damage the paint or even clog up the vent holes in its hood.

Lighting a gas grill and getting it started is easy as long as you follow the manufacturer's instructions. Just be sure that you have enough gas to run it for about another hour.

When cooking, remember that the closer to the hood of the grill you can keep your food, the quicker it will cook and save fuel. For example, if you are grilling steak, then keep the steak on one side of the grill (or use a griddle) instead of placing several steaks directly on top of each other.

The first thing you want to do after cooking your food is to clean the grease from your griddle. Grease from meats can be difficult to remove and you may need a special cleaner for this purpose.

If you are using the outdoor griddle at all four legs, then keep it as stable as possible. Make sure that it is firmly set on a solid surface and level so that it won't tip over easily when you are using it. Closing the lid of an outdoor stove can also help steady the unit so that your food will cook evenly and quickly.

There are a lot of accessories that you'll need with your new grill, but the best one is a cover. Covering your grill will help protect it from environmental hazards such as leaves and tree sap that could damage the paint or even clog up the vent holes in its hood.

I hope you liked this book!

Cooking Temperature

	RARE 135°F/57°C	MEDIUM-RARE 145°F/63°C	MEDIUM 160°F/71°C	MEDIUM-WELL 165°F/74°C
¼ inch	45 seconds	1 minute	2 minutes	3 minutes
½ inch	3 minutes	4 minutes	5 minutes	6 minutes
¾ inch	4 to 5 minutes	6 to 7 minutes	8 to 10 minutes	10 to 12 minutes
1 inch	8 to 10 minutes	10 to 12 minutes	12 to 14 minutes	14 to 16 minutes
1½ inches	14 to 16 minutes	16 to 19 minutes	22 to 26 minutes	26 to 30 minutes
2 inches	18 to 22 minutes	24 to 28 minutes	28 to 32 minutes	33 to 36 minutes

FOOD TYPE	TEMPERATURE
Steak/Beef (Rare)	125° F (52° C)
Steak/Beef (Medium-Rare)	135° F (57° C)
Steak/Beef (Medium)	145° F (63° C)
Steak/Beef (Medium-Well)	150° F (66° C)
Steak/Beef (Well done)	160° F (71° C)
Chicken/Turkey	165° F (74° C)
Ground Poultry	165° F (74° C)
Pork, Veal, Lamb	145° F (63° C)
Ham (precooked)	140° F (60°C)
Fish & Shellfish	145° F (63° C)
Egg Dishes	165° F (74° C)
Leftovers/Casseroles	165° F (74° C)
Stuffing/Dressing	165° F (74° C)
Holding temp for cooked food	140°F (60°C)

Index

Made in the USA
Las Vegas, NV
01 June 2023